THE AMAZING METS

This is the team that has inspired more affection than any other in the history of baseball—probably including even the old Brooklyn Dodgers. From their woeful beginning in 1962 when the Mets lost their first nine games—and went on to lose 120 games for the season—they indicated clearly that they were not the usual run of ballplayers.

But they were amazing in how they could attract more customers in their first season than seven other ball clubs, all of them with higher standings in major leagues. Amazing in the number of ways they managed to lose ball games, repeatedly discovering new ways after they had supposedly exhausted every possible means. And, finally, amazing in how they came off a ninth-place finish the previous year to make the championship of their division, a three-game sweep of the playoff for the National League pennant, and a final, glorious win in the World Series.

Here is the most colorful, most adored, most improbable and now the most successful team in baseball today, lovingly described by the well-known *New York Post* sportswriter, Jerry Mitchell, who has followed the team from its inception, through the dark but entertaining days of their early years, to their present joyous eminence.

You will find the same absorbing reading and high quality in other TEMPO BOOKS. Look for them wherever books are sold. If your dealer does not have the TEMPO BOOKS you want, you may order them by mail, enclosing the list price plus 10¢ a copy to cover mailing.

A complete list of titles is available free from TEMPO BOOKS, Grosset & Dunlap, Inc., 51 Madison Avenue, New York, New York 10010; some of the books you will enjoy are listed in the back of this book.

THE

Amazing
Mets

BY JERRY MITCHELL

Grosset & Dunlap · New York
A NATIONAL GENERAL COMPANY

TEMPO BOOKS EDITION

REVISED PRINTING, MARCH 1970

LIBRARY OF CONGRESS CATALOG CARD NUMBER: 79-106323

All Rights Reserved

TEMPO BOOKS IS REGISTERED IN THE U.S. PATENT OFFICE

TO MIKE

PRINTED IN THE UNITED STATES OF AMERICA

CONTENTS

WHAT'S AMAZING

The Mets were called amazing even in their incubator days, when they had nothing and the big idea was to try to keep it from becoming less. Now, in 1969, seven years, untold innings, countless fumbles and millions of customers later, they were being called more of the same. Everyone agreed the word fit better than an hour-glass corset.

In their infant days they were amazing, perhaps, because they somehow escaped being condemned by the city of New York, chased out of town or sentenced to Outer Mongolia by a magistrate used to long years of success by the rich, powerful Yankees.

The label was pinned on them early in the going by sportswriters like myself, whose papers had condemned them to the club for past sins in print or because the boss rightly figured they could get along like ham and eggs with the manager, Casey Stengel, baseball's blithest spirit.

It made its first appearance that first spring in the club's St. Petersburg training camp, in fact, when Stengel, the man who was to make so much of so little, *i.e.*, the Mets, watched them win their first exhibition game. The Professor, beginning his post-game oration before the writers and a large fringe of old gaffer tourists, exclaimed:

"They're amazing!"

Once again the Ol' Professor was right. They proved amazing, not to say bewildering, in the number of ways they managed to lose ball games, repeatedly discovering new ways after it was supposed they had exhausted every possible means. They had the cunning of those lovable old vaudeville clowns.

At the same time they were amazing in their ability to play winning, head's-up baseball smack in the middle of horrendous losses. They were amazing in their courage no matter how awful their beatings or how long their losing streaks. They never gave onlookers the impression they weren't trying. They, like their fans, never gave up hope.

The Mets were amazing, despite the new records they set at getting beaten, for attracting more customers their first seven years than seven other ball clubs in both leagues, all of them higher in the standings. They were amazing one night in August of 1963, when, after losing 31 out of 40 night games, they just walked out there and beat the pantaloons off the team that won the pennant and the World Series.

They were amazing for the type of fan they attracted, a faithful-to-the-last-gasp kind of guy, capable of incredible vocal accomplishments, who never seemed to get in the least discouraged despite long strings of losing games.

They were amazing for coming alive in New York, a city abandoned as unable to support a big league club by the National League, and a city owned exclusively, when the Giants folded their tents and stole away to San Francisco, by the lordly Yankees. And they were amazing in being 80 per cent the property of one person, sportswoman Joan Payson, who had the old-fashioned love of baseball once bestowed on family-owned clubs.

Mrs. Payson, who had once owned a piece of the New York Giants, hadn't named any of her Greentree Stable horses after her new heroes yet. The delightful names of some of her horses in the past reflected, as you may recall, her passion for baseball, as witness Hall of Fame, Third League, One Hitter and Shut Out. The chances were good, however, that she would some day name one of her better hay-burners Metsie. The horse would, of course, prove amazing.

The years went by as years have a habit of doing, and suddenly, in 1969, the lovable little rascals of Flushing Meadows became big boys with muscles, determination and heretofore hidden skills. They won ball games they weren't supposed to win, even in their dreams. They put New York town, and for that matter the rest of baseball, in a tizzy, for by mid-July they were playing better baseball than the world champion Detroit Tigers of the American League and the defending champion St. Louis Cardinals in the National.

They had the entire National League shocked and the first-place Cubs fearing for their lead. Instead of asking if the Mets Were Bad for Baseball, some were at last asking the speculative question: Will Success Spoil the New York Mets Fans?

Earlier in the season there was some evidence that the town might be getting a bit tired of a team that lost the horrendous total of 737 games in seven years, a little weary of waiting for the Mets to shed their clown's paint. They were running more than 50,000 behind their record home attendance of 1,932,693 set in 1963, when they were such lovable losers, wallowing in ninth place.

Now they were making motions in the direction of the pennant and people couldn't get enough of them. Baseball came suddenly alive again as it hadn't been since the Yankees' days of glory. Fans who couldn't get off for afternoon games began to wear transistor radios like wrist watches, and bars and stores were crowded with others watching their games on television.

When they started their all-important series at Shea with the Cubs there were 37,278 paying customers at the game. There would have been more but the Mets had invited 23,000 kids who took up the other seats. On Wednesday night there were 59,032 paid present. Then the next day there were 49,732.

The Mets' telephone number is NR 2-2000. From early every day—between busy signals—it barked a recorded message: "All reserved and box seats have been sold. Only general admission will go on sale. If you have any questions about any other games call NR 2-2000. Thank you. . . . All reserved and box seats have been sold. Only general admissions etc. etc. etc."

Inside the park the load of telephone calls was so bad that it was impossible even for front office personnel to make a call to the office down the hall. M. Donald Grant, the chairman of the Mets' Board of Directors, couldn't get a call through to his office—or any office. A company, wanting to know how many extra thousand hot dogs, rolls and other fodder the Harry M. Stevens concession people wanted for the expected crowds to come, got nothing but busy signals.

Then there was the mail. "It was piled high everywhere you turned," said Harold Weissman, the Mets' director of public relations. "It's staggering. All we can do is move it from one place to another and get around to opening it as quickly as we can. There are even letters from people who want to BUY tickets. And you can tell how hot we are from the number of requests for free seats. People who ask for free seats never go for a second-class attraction."

After years of losing, of watching them fumble and fool, the fans showed that they loved the Mets just as much when they were winning. There were five paid crowds of more than 50,000 in the National League before the All Star Game break on July 22, and four of them were at Shea Stadium. Attendance zoomed and it didn't seem to need the hypo help of Bat Day, Family Day, Helmet Day, Date Night and Banner Day.

For that matter, Banner Day was almost any day at Shea. Bedsheets with messages exhorting their heroes were all over the place even as they had been in the Polo Grounds and the new home in Flushing Meadows. Many a mattress in Queens, Manhattan, Hempstead, L. I., and elsewhere must have been bare because the artist in every Met fan felt compelled to get paint or shoe polish and spread some message thereon.

One, Karl Eberhardt, of Queens, came to his seat behind third base every game equipped with a satchel of white-on-black posters, which he hoisted for all to see as the occasion demanded. When an opposing player homered, he held up a sign reading "AAARGH!" When a Met rally was needed it was the usual "LET'S GO METS!" When Ed Kranepool hit, the sign read "SUPER-DUPERSTAR!"

"The fans are unbelievable," said pitcher Tom Seaver. "I come from Los Angeles and when somebody on the Dodgers hits a home run there the fans clap politely. Here the noise gets into your system. I feel my heart pounding out there, the adrenalin flowing. It's like being in a wonderful dream."

Sometimes now they booed. Like when Ron Swoboda, a free-swinging throwback to earlier days, tied a record by striking out five times in one game. But the outfielder, who got his share of cheers and cheering banners, understood.

"When you strike out five times," he said, "they should line up along the road and boo you all the way home. Anyway, if we'd lost I'd be eating my heart out. Since we won I'll only chew out one ventricle."

The mood was infectious. "Last season when we were losing I'd feel pretty downcast," said Pitcher Jerry Koosman. "But now, sitting in the dugout and listening to that crowd and all, I always think we'll get 'em before it's over."

Ed Charles, the third baseman, was moved to sing a composition of his own after one particularly stirring victory. He sang:

> East Side, West Side,
> The fans are getting gay.
> After seven long, long years,
> The Mets are on their way.
> South Side, North Side,
> The word is growing 'round.
> When October rolls around,
> The Mets will wear the crown.

When they came back from five runs behind to win a Sunday game from Montreal and then won a Tuesday pulse-throbber from the Cubs in the ninth inning, all the front office help began to run around the locker-room, where the players were trying to act nonchalant. At the height of the excitement Seaver pointed over to Weissman, who, unlike the pitcher, could remember when they only lost those kind of games, and said:

"Somebody call Doc Mauch, the trainer. The man needs a tranquilizer."

How come the one-time patsies of the league became contenders? How did a team that inspired so many hilarious stories become tiger?

"A number of factors," said Seaver, a poised young man. "One is Gil Hodges, the manager. He treats his players like professionals. Another factor has been the success of our rookies—Gary Gentry and Wayne Garrett in particular. When you can add two guys like that to a baseball team it can become significant."

"Hodges has done more for this club than anybody," said veteran pitcher Don Cardwell. "He has instilled in them the belief that they could play better ball and he made sure that they did."

A man asked the retired George Weiss, the man who, as general manager, started the Mets from scratch, whether they had surprised him by their 1969 showing.

"Yes," he said, "though I did say in the spring that this could be the year for the unpredictable because of the way players were moved around the expansion draft, because of players coming and going constantly for military service and because the leagues were each split into two divisions. It looked like a season in which anything could happen."

To many observers the Mets' rise could be traced to the fact that the old power structure in baseball had disappeared. When they split the two leagues into Eastern and Western divisions for the 1969 season, they made it possible for two clubs to win in each league instead of one. A second place team in late July under the new setup, the Mets would have been fourth in a combined 12-team league.

Someone asked Hodges what had turned his troops

on? What had changed them from tabbies to tigers?

"They just decided to turn themselves on," said the manager. "Maybe for the first time they realized it was just as easy to win as to lose—even in the major leagues."

There were a lot of things. Outfielder Cleon Jones was the Mets' leading hitter in 1968 but he batted .297. This time out he was batting more than 50 points higher to lead the league about the time of the All Star Game break. He also became a spectacular player in the field, doing everything well.

Tommie Agee, an American League Rookie of the Year with the Chicago White Sox in 1966, was advertised and recommended as the long-awaited answer to the Mets' desperate need for a centerfielder. Instead he was a bust, hitting only .217, with 103 strikeouts and an 0-for-10 performance on one afternoon.

"I was waiting for Tommie Agee," said Hodges, who argued with the Mets' front office to protect the youngster in the expansion draft after the 1968 season. "I knew what he was capable of doing."

Hodges' faith was more than repaid. Agee, relaxed and effective again at the plate, was hitting in the .285 neighborhood, providing both speed and power in the lead-off spot and giving the team quality protection in centerfield.

The manager had to do considerable shifts in other positions, particularly the infield, and most of the time he came up smelling like roses. Bud Harrelson, the shortstop, was in and out of the lineup, doing his service hitch in small bits, and Gil had to go with Al Weis, the shortstop who got a busted knee from a Frank Robinson slide in the American League two seasons back. At third base he started with Wayne Garrett, who had played his previous four seasons in the minor leagues. He got some heroics from Garrett, and later, when he had to employ

Bobby Pfeil, the 41st third baseman in the history of the club, he got more of the same.

Weis, hitting .196, drove in five runs one day against Pittsburgh. He was later to hit a three-run homer out of Wrigley Field which gave the Mets a 4–1 lead over the Cubs. The homer, off former Met Dick Selma, was only the fourth he had hit in eight major league seasons and the first he had ever hit over a building, even a small one.

"Weis!" exclaimed Cub manager Leo Durocher when mention of the winning blow was made afterwards. "'Weis!" And threw the towel he was holding into the air over his head.

But pitching is still the name of the game and the Mets showed in 1969 that they had a lot of it.

"It's those good young arms," said Rube Walker, the pitching coach, who was a friend of Hodges on the Brooklyn Dodgers. "We're always in the game with Seaver, Koosman and Gentry in particular. When you have three pitchers like that you have three days going for you. When Nolan Ryan, the fastest of them all, gets all right and Jim McAndrews gets straightened out . . . Well, then you have five days you don't have to worry about."

Much of the credit for the rise of the Mets was obviously attributable to Hodges, who put the pieces together and managed with a strong serenity.

Hodges, who served his apprenticeship as manager in Washington after serving as first baseman for the original Mets, was weaned back from the Senators. It was a case of turn-about being fair play since the Mets had given Washington permission to dicker for his services.

In 1968 he guided the Mets to a club record of 72 victories (surpassing the 66 under Wes Westrum), in keeping with the character of his four full seasons in the

Capital, where he won 62, 70, 71 and 76 after finishing out the 1963 campaign as replacement for Mickey Vernon.

When he supervised the Mets' opening of their spring training camp in February 1969 it marked the first time he had worn a Met uniform since he was stricken with a heart attack during a night game with the Braves the previous September 24. He had spent the winter recuperating in St. Petersburg, where he occasionally took in some Florida Instructional League competition in which the Mets were interested.

In mid '69 Gil looked as fit as ever. He weighed 214, a bit more than he should, but blamed that smilingly on Joan Hodges' way with a kitchen.

The Mets, of course, had helped. It made a man feel great to look at the standings of the clubs on July 16 and see his ball club in second place just four games behind the Cubs.

He had a heart murmur all right. The old ticker was murmuring "Mmmmmmmmm . . . nice."

THOSE MAD MAD MET FANS

Casey Stengel standing on the top step of the dugout, turned his back on the field and looked the crowd over as though surprised there were people present.

The Mets were about to go to bat in the first inning and the ancient crumbling Polo Grounds literally rocked with the racket arising from 50,000 fans. He could see women with babies in their arms, a group of elderly men all wearing Mets caps bought at concession stands, soldiers and sailors on leave, ladies in summer furs, gentlemen in soiled T-shirts, kids in Boy Scout and Little League uniforms and boxes occupied by entire families, picnic hampers and thermos jugs at their feet.

Upstairs a ragamuffin band of more than a dozen youngsters, bearing dented bugles, bass drums, ash-cans covers, bongo drums and other assorted noise-makers, paraded loudly along the main aisle of the concrete horse shoe. Leading them, drum-majorette fashion, was a girl with long blonde hair under a baseball cap. She wore tight blue jeans and a bright red jacket and waved a baseball bat for a baton.

Everywhere Casey looked fans were holding up signs, large ones and small ones, signs fashioned of bedsheets, window shades and cardboard, exhorting the team or individual players. Somewhere in the crowd an ancient foghorn moaned at frequent intervals.

"Ebbets Field was never like this," said Casey, a scarred survivor of the celebrated "Daffiness Boys" who played there under Uncle Wilbert Robinson. "Some of these people are maybe a little nutsy, but you gotta like the tremendous support they give you. They sure jazz you up."

During the first two seasons of the Club's existence veteran people-watchers sought to establish the Met fan in some special classification, like wrestling, horror film, cock-fighting or Indianapolis Speedway zealots.

Some press-box sociologists believed them to be converted Yankee fans, fed up with that club's success. Others tabbed them as old Giant fans, old Dodgers fans or just old National League fans who had crawled into the woodwork and disappeared when the Giants left the Polo Grounds and the Dodgers left Ebbets Field.

They were called masochists, joiners, professional wake-goers, adult and juvenile delinquents and people who wanted to join the Foreign Legion but didn't want to go all that distance.

Robert M. Lipsyte, of the New York Times, conferred with some prominent double-domes and came up with this composite portrait of a Mets fan:

The typical Metaphile is five feet eight inches tall, weighs 165 pounds, was 43 years old on his last birthday and has lost considerable hair. He is a skilled laborer with a family, a small apartment and one good suit, which he never wears to the Polo Grounds.

He reported that the typical Yankee fan was, by contrast, the man in the gray flannel suit who respected only

success and viewed the Mets as laughable, disgraceful—
in essence a rabble.

It was generally agreed that Met fans were a fantastic
out-of-this-world lot and that they all loved gallant losers.
They were incredible down-to-the-last-out optimists.
They always hoped for the best and found the Polo
Grounds the best of all possible worlds for their ingrained
optimism.

It was suggested that the Mets might lose their following if they should by some chance become winners.

There was no danger of this during 1962, their maiden
season, for they lost a record 120 games while winning only
40 and never won more than three in a row.

As early as May of their second season, however, they up
and won five in a row and created a new mood among their
followers. They acted as though they expected to make it
six straight and so did their fans.

Then on June 12th the Mets were walloped 3 to 0 by the
Cincinnati Reds. In what might be considered the passion
of loyalty in a moment of anger and frustration, some
hopped-up fans threw garbage on the field. The umpires
threatened to forfeit the game and Casey Stengel had to
make a public plea for peace. Chico Fernandez, the Mets
shortstop, was lustily booed for a fielding error when he
came to bat, and Leonard Koppert, another New York
Times journalist, was moved to observe: ". . . the new
breed of fans turned ugly."

Dick Young, in the New York Daily News, spanked the
disorderly cultists in words like these: "The trouble with
the New Breed is that some of you are starting to believe
your press clippings. You think you're something special,
and maybe you are, but nobody is so special, ever, that he
can take advantage.

"Make noise? Great. Make noise till you get laryngitis.

"Paint signs? Great. Paint signs till you get bursitis.

"But throw things and all that jazz? What sort of slobs are we raising at the Polo Grounds?"

For the record, the Mets, in the first year of their existence, drew 922,530 people through the Polo Grounds turnstiles. That was nearly 300,000 more than the Giants drew in 1957, the last year of that team's tenancy on the banks of the Harlem. The Mets' home attendance was better than Chicago, Milwaukee and Philadelphia in the National League and Baltimore, Boston, Cleveland, Kansas City and Washington in the American.

Over a five-day stretch, beginning with Memorial Day, when the Giants and Dodgers returned to the Polo Grounds, they drew an incredible 197,433. The turnout so moved the new owners they spent more than $10,000 in paid advertisements in metropolitan newspapers thanking the fans for their loyalty.

The decibel output of the Met fan was so high it disturbed some people. Early in the first season a Yankee official, following one of the Mets' weekday games with the Phillies by radio, telephoned an official of the Harry M. Stevens firm, then concessionaires at both parks, to ask, just-between-us-now, weren't the Mets using canned applause?

Assured that the cheering coming out of his set was the real thing, he said, "My gosh, I didn't think 9,000 people could make that much noise."

Soon the Mets were getting attention from unexpected sources. *The New Yorker* magazine, which mentions baseball about as often as Pravda does, sent its Roger Angell over to investigate.

"Suddenly the Met fans made sense to me," wrote Angell. "What we were witnessing was precisely the opposite of the kind of rooting that goes on across the river. This was the losing cheer, the gallant yell for the good try—in contrast to the genteel sounds coming out of Yankee Stadium.

"This was a new recognition that perfection is admirable but a trifle inhuman, that a stumbling kind of semi-success can be so much more warming. Most of all, perhaps, these exultant yells for the Mets were also yells for ourselves and came from a wry, half-understood recognition that there is more Met than Yankee in every one of us. I knew for whom the fog-horn blew; it blew for me."

Charles Collingwood on CBS Radio's *Observation U.S.A.*, devoted an entire broadcast to the genesis of the Met fan. He made comparisons with the admiration felt for Britain when it stood alone after the fall of France in 1940 and declared that Harry Truman's success in 1948 derived from his role as the underdog.

He nixed the theory that Mets followers were actually fans fed up with Yankee success.

"The Mets are the beneficiaries of the Underdog Factor, a powerful nutriment in the building of loyalty," declared Collingwood. "There is something deep in the human psychology which draws us to the underdog, the competitor who doesn't figure to win, whose skills are not commensurate with his goals but which, far from giving up the struggle, fights even harder.

"Thus, to their fans, when the Mets win a game, the joy is even sweeter and when they lose, as they most always do, there is at least the satisfaction of having done valiant battle."

In his syndicated column, Red Smith put his finger on the self-sufficiency of the Met fan: When the Los Angeles Dodgers paid their first visit to the Polo Grounds a fan spotted Vince Scully, a popular young broadcaster in the Ebbets Field era who had been swept along to the Coast in the O'Malley Gold Rush.

"Hey, Vince Scully!" he yelled.

Scully, pleased no end at being recognized after a five-year absence, waved a friendly greeting.

"G'wan back to California, ya' bum ya'l" the fan shouted. "Who needs YOU?"

The fans were something special in many ways. Customers growled elsewhere in baseball about overlong ball games but you heard no such complaints at the Polo Grounds. Win or lose, in daylight or under the kilowatts, they couldn't get enough of their huggable heroes. There were apparently no worries about getting home late for dinner because families attended en masse. It was a love affair without a curfew.

Sunday double-headers found thousands waiting outside on Eighth Avenue for the gates to open. A beating, however one-sided, never dampened their enthusiasm. The hard core remained until the end of the second game, gathering then in front of the centerfield clubhouse to yell some more and demand that some particularly loved one come out and take a bow. If anybody quit before the end of the long day they were pegged as Yankee fans who had come slumming to find out how the other half lived.

The Met fans could take it no matter how awful the errors or the length of a losing streak. Some must have been descendants of the fellow who was reportedly willing to die for dear old Rutgers, or firm believers in the adage that every doormat has a day in the sun. A wicked walloping only brought them back with more and louder hellza-poppin hurrah.

The great number of young people among the fans during the first two seasons was astonishing. Most of the teen-agers you saw couldn't have been more than twelve years old when the Giants and Dodgers lammed out for California, so it couldn't have been a feeling for the "old days."

Possibly the fact that they were given more freedom of movement and expression than at Yankee Stadium had something to do with it. The Mets management encouraged the young signmakers, let them wave their brave banners all over the place and made no attempt to halt the amateur bandsmen who paraded the aisles.

The teen-agers were present in large numbers even at night games during the school term, leading to the suspicion that the kids around the New York area were either great scholars who did their homework successfully between innings or were researching a treatise on baseball. Seeing them stream out of the park with their drums, their horns, and their banners after a game was like watching a crowd leaving a high school football game.

Subway workers found a 28″ x 16½″ bass drum on the platform of the 158th Street station of the Independent Subway late one night. It was taken to the Lost and Found Department along with the umbrellas, sun glasses, lunch pails and empty wallets.

The Mets had lost to the Dodgers that night, their twelfth defeat in succession, so it was thought that the drum had been disdainfully discarded by disgusted young rooters who saw no future in beating it any more for the Mets.

The next day, however, five Brooklyn high school students showed up to claim the drum. It developed that in the confusion of the post-game subway rush the boys got separated and misplaced their drum.

"Each of us figured that one of the other guys had it," explained one boy at a press conference deemed necessary for such a momentous occasion. "We were heartbroken until we read in the papers that it had been turned in. We take turns. It's the loudest drum in the Polo Grounds."

At times it must have seemed as though one out of every

20 fans carried a bedsheet or a window shade and the makings of a sign into the park with him.

Sometimes the lettering was changed a couple of times during a game. Youngsters spread their canvases on the wide aisles or on the floor of the washrooms and went to work with paint, crayon or laundry ink. It seemed as if the bedsheet Botticellis could manufacture signs faster than a newspaper could turn out new editions.

The first sign anyone remembers appeared in July of the first season, when Marv' Throneberry was working hard to become the symbol of the club. It read: "Cranbury, Strawberry, We Love Throneberry."

It was catching. A few days later five youths climbed on top of the Mets' dugout during a game. Four of them carried a large block letter apiece and the fifth an exclamation point. Lined up facing the stands they spelled out the object of their affection.

"M A R V!"

House cops soon corraled the five and escorted them from the park. A few innings later, however, they were seen holding their letters high in the left centerfield bleachers. Throneberry, among other distinctions, must be the only ball player in history for whom customers paid two admissions to watch.

Soon signs began to bloom all over the park at every game. They included not only countless, "Let's Go Mets" but others reading, "Our Mom Loves the Mets," "For Rookie of the Year—Casey Stengel," "Mike's Diner Digs the Mets," and "World Series Tickets Sold Here."

Also an extra-large banner that read:

"M is for Mighty
E is for Exciting
T is for Terrific
S is for So Lovable"

"We must have some of the most literate fans in the country," remarked the Mets' promotion director, Tom Meany, as he scanned the crowd one afternoon.

"Over there's a sign that says 'Chastise Those Cincinnatians,' and over there one says, 'Press on Metropolitans.'"

Naturally the club decided to hold a Banner Day, being careful to select a September Sunday that wouldn't conflict with the Greenwich Village Outdoor Art Exhibit or any such affair. Between games of a double-header with the Houston Colts, the centerfield exit was opened and 400-odd sign-makers and carriers who had been assembling outside for hours, marched slowly in. One by one, two by two and four by four, they marched around the field and out again as a record screeched "Strike Up the Band" over the public address system.

Their signs bore such legends as, "O'Malley Is a Fink. May His Dodgers Sink, Sink, Sink," "Up A Tree in '63, Off The Floor In '64," "Hit One Into The Darkness, Harkness," "Hickman for President," "Know Why The Mets are Such Good Losers?—Practice Makes Perfect," and some in Spanish.

Myron Meisner, an 18-year-old Bronxite who had carried a "Let's Go Stengel Lancers" banner about the park all season, switched to one that merely read, "This Sign in Favor Of The Mets," for the big day.

When the exit gates had closed on the last of them the clubhouse door opened and down the steps came the Mets, each carrying a white cardboard about two feet high and two feet wide. They lined up in centerfield, marched in about as far as second base in a reasonable facsimile of a straight line, then stopped and, at a signal from Field Marshall Jules Adler, turned placards for all to read:

"TO THE METS FANS—WE LOVE YOU TOO."

Then, out of the dugout, bearing another placard,

came Casey Stengel. He jogged to the end of the line, turned and showed an exclamation point.

"Beautiful, simply beautiful," exclaimed a Mets addict.

"Ghastly," a visiting Yankee fan answered with a shudder.

Perhaps the most enjoyable game of the first two seasons for many Met fans took place not at the Polo Grounds but at Yankee Stadium. That was the Mayor's Trophy game, an exhibition affair for the benefit of sandlot baseball around New York. The Mets wore the gray uniforms prescribed for visitors and took their batting practice first, but they could have been mistaken for the home team, so loudly were they cheered. Their 6–2 victory over the Yankees was acclaimed by the crowd of 50,000.

Before the game Met fans were practically frisked at the gate, by house cops who took away the home-work of the sign-makers before admitting them.

"Where ya' think yar, anyways, the Polo Grounds?" was frequently heard as the Mets enthusiasts were deprived of their banners of love.

The coppers didn't frisk far enough, however, for firecrackers, torpedos, cherry bombs and rockets exploded on the field and in the stands all during the game. One rocket, leaving a trail of flame and smoke as it tailed down from the upper stands, exploded between home plate and the pitcher's mound. A large firecracker that exploded at his feet made Vinnie Smith, the first-base umpire, wish he had taken the night off.

Fights broke out as thousands milled about in centerfield after the game. The busy house cops dashed into the crowd and effected some captures. Some fans tried to tear down the Yankees' championship banner, probably with the idea of decorating the Polo Grounds with it. More firecrackers popped here and there in the crowd.

A group of teen-agers pranced down the third base foul line with a dummy in a Yankee uniform. The effigy bore No. 35, signifying Ralph Houk, the Yankee manager. "They yelled when Joe Pepitone hit his home run, didn't they?" said Houk, secure in the clubhouse afterwards. "I was surprised. Up to then, judging from the noise, I didn't think there were any Yankee fans in the place. No, it wasn't too bad. I really expected it to be worse."

"Better not leave the park yet," someone advised, as the Yankees finished dressing for the street. "You'll get mobbed out there."

So they waited an extra hour, sipping their beer and talking of the carnival crowd and the noisiest night they had ever experienced. They could still hear the chanting outside:

"Yankees, go home!"

Not all the Met fans were beardless youths with a bugle in one hand and a sign in the other. The oldsters who had forgotten about baseball when the Giants and Dodgers fled to California welcomed them. Old gaffers who had watched the Giants of John McGraw, Bill Terry, Mel Ott and Lippy Durocher, returned to their favorite pews. Others who had known no other park than Ebbets Field, decided that the Polo Grounds was a worthwhile place to visit after all, now that the National League was in business there again.

Ushers from the old days, working in the park again, recognized former regulars among the customers. Old groups reformed, including surviving members of the Section Thirty Club, consisting of night club entertainers, musicians, waiters, stage-hands, song writers, bartenders, doormen, bus boys and other night people who had occupied the upstairs section behind third base for many years. The Section Thirty Club membership had included such Broadway and West 52nd Street characters as Jack White, Pat Harrington, Eddie Duchin, Don Weatherston, Jerri Blanchard, Sam Dody, Jack Loeffler, Jimmy Durante, Sammy Sachs, Broadway Sam Roth, Bob Broderick, Fred Allen, Toots Shor, Freddie Lamb, Harry Ruby, Fred Waring, Eddie Davis, Benny Rubin, Picadilly Charley Gehrig and Bill Bojangles Robinson. A roll call at any Mets' game would have shown that many members had departed from this green footstool but there were still a goodly lot of them in their old seats.

The Section Five Club also returned to life with the coming of the Mets, its members taking over their old upstairs sections behind right field. In the days of the Giants the members used to welcome the ball players back from spring training with a pre-season social in the Concourse Plaza Hotel, then get together for another big affair after the season ended.

The sun-bathers of the Solarium Club, formed in early Giant years by Meyer Cohen, a department store executive, were also happy to see the old homestead again. They found their old seats in Section Thirty-three, stripped to their waists and once more enjoyed the sun and, at times, the way the home troops played ball.

You were also apt to find the sixty-odd members of the Senior Citizens Club from the Red Hook section of Brooklyn, ranging in age from 70 to 104, at a Mets game now and then. They formerly made their baseball pilgrimages to Ebbets Field. In fact, a number of them remembered watching Casey Stengel *play* there. At their first game at the Polo Grounds they presented Casey with a softball and bat, which may or may not have been a form of criticism.

The Mets found fans everywhere they went. They became sentimental favorites all over baseball, people rooting for their home team first and the Mets next.

The interest in them outside of New York was staggering. Bartenders in Chicago asked about the Mets. Barbers in St. Louis wanted all the details of their losing streaks. Waitresses in Detroit wanted to know what manner of men they were. In Los Angeles, a taxi-driver, hustling people from the airport, said:

"You from New York? Thought so. Say, how about those Mets, huh? Imagine them beatin' the Dodgers. Boy, too bad O'Malley didn't see that one. Him an' his big, fat cigar. That old Casey Stengel's all right, all right."

Signs pleading, "Let's Go Mets," popped up in Houston, Philadelphia, San Francisco and Cincinnati when the Mets played in those cities. Some were hoisted by touring American Youth Hostel groups from New York and New Jersey, and others doubtlessly by whimsical-minded tourists or fans who just wanted to needle other home fans.

One night in Forbes Field, Pittsburgh, a troup of teen-agers paraded bravely through the stands with Mets banners throughout a game.

"We're members of a sandlot team in the East Liberty section," one of them explained, "and we're not very good ourselves. That's why we like the Mets. We keep tryin' but we keep losin'."

Letters from Met fans were a daily deluge at the Polo Grounds and the club's Fifth Avenue office. Among those heard from practically every day of the week was Joseph Landsman, who described himself as the Mets' poet laureate. Mr. Landsman also contributed heavily to the mail of most of the New York sportswriters every day, each letter usually containing three or four handwritten pages. When he got tired or went into a slump, he sent postcards.

When Duke Snider was shopping for the 400th home run of his major league career, the poet Landsman was inspired to dash this one off between innings of a game:

"This is it, One More Blow
Down in history you will go.
With Ruth, Gehrig, Foxx, and Ott
Never will they be forgot.
 (Williams, Musial, Mantle, Mathews are in it too.)
Come on Duke, we're rooting for you."

It was the evening of April 23rd, 1962, and the fight
crowd in the St. Nicholas Arena, New York, stirred im-
patiently as Johnny Addie, the tuxedo-clad announcer,
collected the slips from the judges and referee which were
to show that Rickey Ortiz had won the featured eight-
round bout from Billy Bello. Howie Smith, the Western
Union operator beckoned to Addie, then whispered something as the announcer bent over the ropes.

"Ladies and gentlemen," said Addie, when he took the
microphone at the center of the ring afterwards, "before
I divulge to you the name of the winnah of tonight's stel-
lar attraction, the just concluded eight-round feature bout
between Rickey Ortiz, that sensational lightweight battler
from Puerto Rico, and Billy Bello, the always popular
pride of the Bronx, I would like to give you the latest
baseball news brought to you by Western Union telegraph
direct from Pittsburgh, Pennsylvania, courtesy of the St.
Nick Arena, which is aware of your keen interest in the
fortunes of that great baseball team—the New York Mets.

"At the end of six innings in Pittsburgh, Pennsylvania,
the score is New York Mets six, the Pittsburgh Pirates,
nothing. . . And now. . . ."

Cheers, equal in volume to any that had ever been heard
in that ancient slaughter house, came from a crowd which
apparently appreciated the underdogs in baseball as much
as in boxing.

It was the morning of October 23, 1962. President John
F. Kennedy had the night before declared an embargo on

Cuba, taking a step which could have meant the beginning of thermo-nuclear war. There was a sense of crisis all over the United States and all over the world.

In the quiet little village of Cooperstown, N. Y., far from the centers of anxiety but feeling the impact nevertheless, Lee Allen, historian of the Baseball Hall of Fame, sat at his desk. He was thinking that if the Russians picked up the challenge it might very well mean the end of life as we know it. Brooding over the future, Lee attacked his mail. He turned over a postcard from New York's Bronx, and read:

"Dear Sir:

What was the record of the New York Mets this year on Thursdays? I would appreciate a game-by-game total. Thank you."

The preposterous postcard pulled him right out of his depression. He suddenly realized that, to the Met fan anyway, crises were commonplace. Somehow the card made him feel a lot better.

"My first impulse was to toss it into the waste basket," related Allen. "But it occurred to me that the writer must have had a purpose in asking the question, as unusual a one as I ever received. I checked the records and found that the work of the Mets on Thursdays showed no victories and 15 defeats.

After replying to the fan Allen forwarded the postcard to the Mets with the observation, "With the world on the verge of ruin, I thought you might be interested in what the Mets' fans are worried about."

OL' CASE'

Among the high society events of 1963, ranking right up there with the debutante cotillions and the Firemen's Ball, was a dinner at the swank Regency Hotel on New York's Park Avenue given by Perle Mesta, the hostess with the mostest in Washington, London, Paris and the grand duchy of Luxemburg. It preceded a night game between the New York Mets and the San Francisco Giants. The party was for the wives of the Mets players.

Perle had been giving similar affairs and gushing over them afterward in "Perle Mesta's Party Notebook," her column in *McCall's*. The dinner followed hard on the heels of a Mesta party for the wives of United Nations bigwigs.

As cocktails were being passed around, Betty King of the Mets office explained that Mrs. Casey Stengel couldn't be present since unfortunately she was still at home in California.

"Indeed," boomed the hostess, "and who is Casey Stengel?"

This would seem to suggest that Perle's newspaper read-

ing had been confined to the society columns, since Casey
Stengel had been such a world personality for so many
years that possibly only a couple of dozen people in Lower
Cambodia had not yet heard the name.

When the Regency clambake was over, the whole crowd,
including Perle, a *McCall's* photographer and a hootenanny singer, went out to the Polo Grounds. They
watched the Mets beat the Giants in the eleventh, 9-7, on
a home run by Joe Hicks.

There was a reception afterward in the Directors'
Room, which is deep in the bowels of the Polo Grounds
between the H. M. Stevens frankfurter vault and the
beer bin. Casey Stengel, who must have heard echoes of
Perle Mesta's party, was there, of course. When he saw Al
Dark, manager of the defeated Giants, come into the
room, he bellowed for all to hear:

"Now, isn't that nice of Mr. Dark, after losin' a tough
ball game an' all, to come in here to this party bein' given
by that . . . Mrs. What's-Her-Name?"

Casey knew the lady's name. Those around him are convinced the man knows everything—from the reason why a
certain pitcher was unable to keep the ball low in a Sunday
game (he pitched too many highballs Saturday night) to
the contents of the Indonesian Oil Agreement, from the
lineup of the Newark International League club of 1915
to the workings of magnetohydrodynamics. On practically
any subject Casey would take his listeners on such a journey of words they would come away convinced he had
given them the answer somewhere along the way; they
just hadn't caught it on the right bounce.

"I listened to him talk non-stop for 45 minutes," a certain doctor from New Bedford admits, having met Casey
on a Florida vacation. "I haven't the slightest idea what he
was talking about, but I was never so beguiled in all my
life."

Casey Stengel first made himself heard in the delivery room of a Kansas City hospital the morning of July 30, 1890. His father was of German descent, his mother Irish. He was born Charles Dillon Stengel and never was certain how he acquired the "Casey." It might have come from "K.C.," the familiar abbreviation for his home town, he says, or because "Casey at the Bat" was a popular rendition during his playing days. In his boyhood they called him "Dutch."

His brother Grant, two years older, was a better ball player, according to Casey, and would have been a major leaguer but for a foot accident. The boys went to Central High and played on the football and baseball teams. Casey was also a basketball guard at Central.

When he wasn't helping his father and brother operate a sprinkling cart, or working as delivery boy for a florist, Casey was usually playing baseball. The first money he earned from the game was for pitching for the Parisian Cloak Company team. Grant got him on the Armour & Company team and later the Northeast Merchants.

Famous in his later managing years as a platooner, Casey thinks a liking for such maneuvering evolved in his youth. He won a job as a third baseman, then switched to second base a year later when the team came up with a better third baseman. In his third year in high school he became a pitcher.

In 1910 Central won the state baseball championship, beating Joplin 7–6 in 15 innings with Casey pitching. The Kansas City club, then in the American Association, had a scout at the game and signed him for the 1910 season.

Casey gives credit to a number of men for helping him in his early years, men like Charles Augustus "Kid" Nichols, who had pitched for Boston, St. Louis and Philadelphia of the National League and had also managed the Cardinals.

"He lived across the street from us," recalls Casey, "and when he heard I'd signed with the Blues he called me over and gave me some advice that I later often gave my own players.

"The first thing you should do," he told me, "is listen all the time to your manager and the older players. Never disregard their advice or say you won't do what they tell you to do. Memorize their advice. And when you can, ask them to teach you things to better your play."

Casey went to the Kansas City training camp that next spring as a pitcher but got clobbered time and again. He finally told them that he was really an outfielder, but his inexperience showed when he tried to turn around and try for balls over his head. The Blues left him behind when they went on their first road trip. They also left behind two older players, who went to work on the youngster.

"One was Spike Shannon," relates Casey. "He had played the outfield for the Cardinals, Pirates and the New York Giants. He'd take a chair into the outfield with him, sit down and yell what I was to do, what I did wrong an' what I did right.

"The other was Pat Flaherty, who had pitched for the Cubs, Pirates an' Phillies. He would take a bat an' hit balls over my head or just out of reach to the left or right. They kept this up every day until the Blues came back from their trip—I was doin' much better.

"Flaherty taught me one other thing. He used to pitch to me after my lessons in the outfield were over, and this one day I let a ball go by an' then stood there lookin' down at the plate. As soon as he got the ball back Flaherty quick-pitched it while I was still dreamin' and hit me right in the belly, knockin' me flat.

" 'That'll teach you to always keep your eye on the ball,' he told me."

Finally Kansas City sent the 19-year-old Stengel to Kan-

kakee of the Northern Association for some needed seasoning. Flaherty advised him, as he left, not only to con-
tinue to practice fielding but also to practice sliding.

At Kankakee Casey had a teammate hit balls over his
head the way Flaherty had. Then, after throwing the ball
back, he would drop his glove on the grass for a "base"
slide into it both right and left until his helper was ready
to hit another fly.

They thought he was daft.

"That Stengel is one guy who won't be with us long,"
predicted a veteran.

"You mean he's goin' up to the big leagues?" asked
another.

"No, I mean guys with butterfly nets are gonna' come
out here some day and bag him for that big place over
there," he replied, pointing to the state mental hospital
out behind the centerfield fence.

"They couldn't understand that I was teaching myself,"
explains Casey. "I knew at my age, which was only 19,
that I'd have to beat out a lotta' more experienced players
to get a job an' pay my bills at Western Dental College.

"They saw me sweatin' out there under the hot sun,
catchin' fly balls, throwin', runnin' an' practicin' up on
my sliding. I was practicin' four things at once."

The extra rehearsals paid off. When Kansas City sent
him to Aurora of the Wisconsin-Illinois League next season he led the league in hitting with a .352 average, and in
stolen bases, with 50. Larry Sutton, a scout for the Brooklyn Dodgers, watched him and recommended that he be
drafted. The Dodgers did so after the close of the season
and sent Casey to Montgomery of the Southern Association, with whom they had a working agreement in 1913.

At Montgomery Casey met another man who was to
help improve his play. He was Kid Elberfeld, the shortstop, a tough veteran of 14 years in the major leagues.

"He was good to me," Casey recalls. "He'd say, 'You want to make it big? You want to go up to Brooklyn? Well just watch me.'

"He worked with me so I'd execute the different plays better, the hit an' run an' so forth. I could run good, an' he'd have me take a big lead off second base so the shortstop would have to move over. Then I would light out for third so the third baseman would have to cover that base an' then he'd hit the ball through the big hole they'd left.

"He was great at gettin' hit by a pitched ball, like Hughie Jennings of the Giants an' later on Frank Crosetti of the Yankees. He'd get in the way of a pitch an' sometimes just so the umpire wouldn't think he had done it on purpose, he'd throw that short bottle bat of his at the pitcher an' yell, 'You threw at me on purpose, you no good so-n'-so!' "

When Brooklyn yoohooed for Casey late in the season, Elberfeld refused to let him leave their Montgomery rooming house with the old cardboard suitcase he'd been carrying.

" 'That suitcase is a thousand-miler, but only if the weather's good,' he told me," recalls Stengel. " 'If you got caught in the rain you'd be holdin' only a handle. Go out an' buy a good leather bag. You go up the big leagues you gotta go up in style.' He also made me buy wine for the fellows in the club who were seein' me off at the railroad station."

Casey's baseball education continued. When he reported to the Brooklyn clubhouse a group of merry Dodgers was sharing a bucket of suds that the clubhouse man had fetched from a nearby saloon. A dice game was going on in one corner. Casey watched for a while, then wanting to appear to be one of the boys, he got into the game himself.

The bones were still rolling when manager Bill Dahlen walked in. After dressing down the others he took Stengel aside.

"You come up here to gamble or to play ball?" he asked.

"To play ball," answered Casey.

"Then get into your uniform an' get out on the field an' show me," he roared. "We didn't bring you up from the minors to shoot craps!"

Soon Zach Wheat, the outfielder from Kansas City, was helping him as Flaherty and Shannon had.

"Wheat was a wonderful hitter," says Casey, "line drive after line drive, an' he had been in the league an' knew all the parks an' hitters. I remember he advised me to play back the first time Hans Wagner came to bat when we played Pittsburgh.

" 'I'm pretty far back now,' I said.

" 'Get further back!' he yelled.

"I went back another good six or eight feet an' Wagner hit the ball right over my head in centerfield."

As he had from older players, Casey learned much from his managers. From Bill Dahlen and Uncle Wilbert Robinson in Brooklyn, Gavvy Cravath and Wild Bill Donovan in Philadelphia, Hugo Bezdek in Pittsburgh and John McGraw of the New York Giants. A little of each great man rubbed off on Stengel.

"I thought I was pretty good as a base-runner an' slider when I came up to Brooklyn," Casey tells it, "because I'd led entire leagues in stealin' in the minors. But Dahlen improved me. He showed me how to slide in, just touch the base an' then spring right up fast ready to go on to third, just like Ross Youngs of the Giants, who was an amazin' base-runner.

"It was fun to play for Uncle Robbie. There were laughs in the clubhouse an' laughs on the bench with him around. We'd start an argument about farm products or huntin' dogs or corn likker an' first thing you know Robbie'd be right in the middle of it, like one of the players.

"He was what you'd call a good con man; he'd make you think he thought you were a better ball player than you were. He platooned me, taking me out against the very good lefthanded pitchers, since I had some trouble with them as a lefthanded hitter. But he did it smart. He just liked to keep you feelin' good.

"He was a great manager with pitchers, an' the bigger they were the better he liked them. That was probably because he used to be a catcher, I suppose. He was also great at gettin' good seasons out of old pitchers who were supposed to be all washed up.

"Hugo Bezdek had never played big league ball but he knew the game an' he was smart. He'd been football coach at Penn State an' a great one, an' he took over the management of the Pirates more or less as a favor to Barney Dreyfuss, the owner.

"Bezdek taught me how to find out things I wasn't sure of, an' to use the knowledge of men who might know more about somethin' than I did. He used to hold meetings an' ask his experienced players questions. He'd ask a man who'd come from the Chicago Cubs in a trade how Frank Chance, the Chicago manager, did things. He'd ask Max Carey, a great base-runner, to explain his ideas on stealin'. And he'd ask Billy Hinchman, a very fine hitter, what about the percentages for an' against sluggin' an' place-hittin'.

"When I was with the Phillies later I was under Gavvy Gravath and then Wild Bill Donovan. Cravath was a good teacher of hitting an' he helped me there. Donovan had been a great pitcher in his Detroit years an' he knew how to teach it an' how to handle pitchers an' I learned from him.

"The greatest manager I played for—no question about it—was McGraw. He was also the strictest an' a manager who told you off in language you'd remember better than the others.

"He always wanted every play executed properly an' no alibis. If you couldn't execute after three or four tries he'd decide that you were either too dumb or too awkward to play for him.

"Then he would trade you. But if you improved he would probably get you back. He didn't stay stubbornly with his first opinion. He always traded with the thought, 'I can buy this man back if he gets better an' he can help me win.'"

"He made you make the big effort, made you put out all the time. He wanted you to fight the ball, not just stand there. He was good at startin' double steals, at seein' that his men ran the bases alertly. He was a wonderful manager, particularly offensively. And no manager adapted his game better from the dead ball we used to play with to the lively ball we use today."

Casey made enough money his first two years in baseball to pay his tuition at dental college after the season, but when he zoomed up to Brooklyn in his third year he decided to forget about dentistry and concentrate on baseball.

"I would say some strange things happened when I was studying to be a lefthanded dentist," said Casey. "Like the first time I tried to pull a tooth of one of the free patients we practiced on an' I forgot to lower the chair an' then pulled instead of twistin' first an' the fella come leapin' outa the chair. After that I practiced on my relatives."

In his first game as a Dodger he got four straight hits off Claude Hendrix, the league's leading pitcher. When he went up to bat for the fifth time he found Sherry Smith, a lefthander, had replaced Hendrix.

"All right, you bush phenom', let's see you cross over the other side of the plate!" yelled Fred Clarke, the Pittsburgh manager.

"An' I was cocky an' nutsy enough to do it," said Casey. "So I stand there righthanded an' what do I do but get a base on balls.

"We played an exhibition game in Newark later on in the season an' they had a contest to see who could catch a greased pig before the game. Six or seven of us go after the pig an' we were fallin' all over the place. Once I got a good hold of him by his rear legs. He eventually got away but they said I'd held him the longest so I got the prize."

The first time rookie Stengel played for the Dodgers in the Polo Grounds, he hit three line drives that were caught. McGraw, coming out to the coaching box, stopped him after the third robbery.

"I have to hand it to you, kid," he said. "You look like the best hitter on that Brooklyn club."

"Gee thanks, Mr. McGraw," said Casey, highly pleased at being rated over such hitters as Wheat and Jake Daubert by such an authority.

"But remember," added McGraw, "the club just had that wall built, so don't you go runnin' into it with that billiard ball head of yours."

On the Dodgers Casey later became the leader of a group that always wound up at the same saloon after a game to gripe about the umpires, the front office, the owners, the bad job the groundskeeper was doing and Uncle Robbie's mistakes.

"Holy smoke, we're in for it," the bartender would yell as they came into the joint. "Here come The Grumblers!"

One spring the Dodgers played an exhibition game in Pensacola, Fla., and when Casey went out to his center-field position he noticed a large steel manhole cover. He lifted one edge of it and saw there was a hole about four feet deep with a pipe and a faucet in it used for watering the field. In one of the late innings, when everyone was watching a change of pitchers, he lifted the cover and jumped down in the hole, holding the cover up just enough to see what was going on.

"Somebody hit a fly ball to centerfield," relates Casey, "an' I knew everybody must be suprised not to see any outfielder there. Then I flipped off the cover an' jumped out and grabbed the ball. I would say the customers were shocked that day."

The Dodgers traded Casey to Pittsburgh after the 1917 season. When he played at Ebbets Field in Brooklyn for the Pirates the first time, the fans began to ride him as soon as he appeared. He had been visiting pitcher Leon Cadore, one of his old Brooklyn buddies, in the bullpen before coming into the bench, and when the customers began to hoot at him again, Casey winked and told his Pirate teammates, "Just watch."

When he walked up to the plate for the first time, swinging three bats, the booing grew in volume. Casey lifted his hand to Umpire Cy Rigler and called time. Then he dropped the bats, bowed low to the assembled multitude and lifted his cap. Out flew a sparrow.

"You shoulda' heard that crowd," recalled Casey. There was one big startled wow!—and a few complaints to the club afterward about what they said was a smart-alecky stunt. He had got the sparrow from Cadore who had just caught it in the bullpen.

"I guess that's remembered more than anything about my playin' days in Brooklyn."

In 1924, Casey after 12 years in the majors, was traded to Boston by McGraw and he says it was about this time that he started thinking seriously of managing a club. The previous season he had met the girl he wanted to marry,

Edna Lawson of Glendale, and knew that a manager's job would be one way of earning more money and maybe establishing a future after his playing days.

He had been a manager of sorts that previous spring. The Giants always split their squad into two teams after finishing their time at a spring training base and both would play a schedule of exhibition games on the road north.

McGraw, who always took the first squad, approached Stengel before it was time to break camp.

"How'd you like to become a coach some day?" he asked. "You would? Well, I'll try an' help you. I'm gonna' keep Jimmy O'Connell that rookie outfielder with me to see what he can do in centerfield. I already know what you can an' cannot do. So you take the second team an' manage it on the way north."

"I went along with the offer," said Casey "Then I got traded to Boston an' Edna an' I got married an' a year later I started to manage."

That was in May of 1925, when Judge Emil Fuchs, the Boston owner, decided to buy the Worcester club of the Eastern League for a farm on which to develop young players. He named Stengel manager and club president.

Casey liked the dual job but decided that he liked better an offer to manage Toledo, of the American Association. Fuchs being unwilling to let him go, Casey took off his uniform, left the field for the club office, sat in the president's chair and fired himself as a manager through a letter, a copy of which was duly forwarded to a startled Commissioner of Baseball. It read:

> *Manager Casey Stengel is hereby and as of this date dismissed as manager of the Worcester Eastern League club. Signed: Charles Dillon Stengel, President, Worcester Baseball Club.*

The next year, 1926, Casey became manager of the Toledo club of the American Association, after having been recommended by McGraw. He held the job for six years. Then in 1932 he was back in Brooklyn again, this time as a coach under Max Carey. When Max got the boot as manager in 1935, Casey took over as a major league manager for the first time. He didn't agree to take over, however, until assured that Carey would be fully paid for the remaining year of his contract.

A rubber-armed pitcher named Van Lingle Mungo, catcher Al Lopez and infielders Tony Cuccinello, Linus Frey and Buddy Hassett were about the only quality players he possessed in his three Brooklyn years. The rest were worn veterans unwanted by other clubs or youngsters with little experience and often less ability, plus an occasional character carried on the payroll at the insistence of one of the club directors.

It was a musical comedy outfit. One director was a movie executive who spent most of his time in Hollywood. Another was a hat manufacturer whose knowledge of the game would easily have slipped under a skullcap. A third was a fellow who had once pitched for Yale. He liked to show the pitchers, young and old, what was wrong with their deliveries.

Some odd Dodgers played—after their fashion—during those three years. One was Frenchy Bordagaray, an infielder-outfielder who could run extra fast, particularly against a third base coach's stop signals.

Bordagaray reported one spring wearing a mustache and a full-blown goatee, a beatnik ahead of his time. Casey didn't mind the added foliage at first, since it led to more newspaper space, but when they broke camp for the trip home he told Frenchy to get clean-shaven in a hurry.

"It got so he was tryin' to trap ground balls in that goatee," Casey recalls, "He had enough trouble fielding balls with his hands. Besides he ran faster with the fur off."

Then there was Walter Beck, a pitcher tattooed so much by hitters he quickly earned the nickname of Boom Boom. Casey started him in the Phillies' bandbox park one day and hoped for the best. Soon enough the Phils began to boom his pitches against and over the right field wall upholstered with sheet metal. Casey went to the mound to remove him but Beck begged to be left in.

"Nope, I've had enough," Casey told him, beckoning to the bullpen for another pitcher. "Gimme that ball."

Infuriated, Beck turned instead and threw the ball into right field. It went all the way and hit the tin fence with a resounding bang and dropped to the field.

Hack Wilson, the right fielder, grossing 230 pounds, had been standing there with his head down thinking sad thoughts when he was shocked by the sound of the ball hitting the fence. Thinking some batter had whacked it, he turned around, chased it madly and threw it into second base.

As the crowd rocked with laughter Beck returned to the dugout followed by Stengel.

"I'da left you in there," said Casey sourly, "if I had known you could throw as hard as you did to hit that fence."

The Giant-Dodger rivalry was what Casey would call a treeee-mendous thing in those days. Bill Terry had won the pennant and World Series with his 1933 Giants and when he came to the winter meetings in New York, the writers wanted his ideas on the 1934 race. What, asked one, about Brooklyn?

"Brooklyn?" answered Terry, thinking he would make with a little joke. "Is Brooklyn still in the league?"

This carbolic crack, repeated by visiting fans at Ebbetts Field, led to more arguments and fights than the rivalry had ever known before. The Dodger fans considered the score evened, however, when their heroes went up to the Polo Grounds on the last day of the season and knocked the Giants out of a possible pennant.

Almost as many homemade signs filled the Polo Grounds as in the latter days of the Mets. Carried by Brooklyn fans, they read, "Beat the Giants, the bums!" and "Is Brooklyn still in the League? And How!"

While the Cardinals, who had been tied with them for first place, won two games from Cincinnati, the Dodgers beat the Giants, 5–1, behind big Mungo, and then took the second game, 8–5.

It took Stengel more than four hours afterward to get from the Polo Grounds to his Brooklyn hotel. Fans, waiting outside the clubhouse, hoisted him on their shoulders when he tried to leave and carried him down the street and into the subway. Roisterers filled the banner-bedecked cars and their leaders made appropriate speeches. The players made speeches. Stengel made speeches. The train went from Harlem to the end of the line in deepest Brooklyn, then all the way back to the Bronx and to Brooklyn again before Casey was able to escape at Borough Hall and get to the St. George Hotel.

Stengel's teams finished sixth, fifth and seventh in that order his three Brooklyn years, the last in 1936, and the daffy Dodger directorate decided that another managerial change was in order. They reasoned that, while they couldn't buy players or cultivate a farm system that would develop any players, they might be able to appease the fans by bringing in a new manager.

Casey was paid off for 1937 during the 1936 World Series, the idea being that his newspaper friends would be too busy writing about the games to get very angry about the heave ho. Since Casey had been paid for not managing in 1934 and Burleigh Grimes went on the payroll to succeed Stengel in 1937, the Brooklyn club set some sort of a record by paying six managerial salaries in four years.

It developed that Casey's newspaper friends were not too busy at all. The Brooklyn club was roasted in print. Casey was hired by a newspaper syndicate to write about the Series and his friends tossed him a party at the Hotel New Yorker when it was over.

The affair, which attracted some 200 people, was supposed to be strictly a newspaper party but many others demanded tickets. This included a big Yankee delegation, headed by General Manager George Weiss, who was to sign him as Yankee manager twelve years later, and Manager Joe McCarthy.

The sportswriters took turns denouncing the Brooklyn directors from the dias and Stout Steve Owen, coach of the football Giants got up to say: "I've been to a lot of dinners. Dinners for men who had wonderful years and dinners for men who were just well liked, but this is the first dinner I ever heard of honoring a man for getting fired."

In 1937 Casey used most of the $15,000 he got for not managing the Dodgers to go into the oil business. He went into partnership with Randy Moore, who had been a hard-hitting outfielder for the Boston Braves, and the two toured the East Texas oil fields, investing in a number of wells. By that time Moore had persuaded a number of his former Boston teammates, including Al Lopez, Johnny Cooney and Fred Frankhouse, to join them.

Bob Quinn, who had been his general manager the first two years in Brooklyn before moving to take the same post with the Boston Braves, offered Casey the manager's job there. He took over in 1938, succeeding Bill Mc-Kechnie, who had moved on to the Cincinnati Reds.

He stayed on that job for six years and, like his three in Brooklyn, they were pretty lean ones. The club was always heavily populated with poor ball players or, as Casey called them, "road apples."

The Braves finished sixth and Stengel finished with a bad leg in 1943, his last Boston year. He was walking to his hotel in the rain one night with a newspaper held over his head when he was hit by an automobile. He suffered a badly broken leg and was in the hospital for several months. For a time it was thought that amputation might be necessary.

Stengel made many friends in Boston, but he had one caustic critic in a Boston sports writer.

This character called on the people of Boston to honor the man who had run down Stengel in his car, thus depriving the club of his services as manager for more than two months. He asked that an appropriate medal be struck and the driver be presented with it by Mayor Curley on the steps of City Hall as, "the man who did the most for baseball in Boston in 1943."

"But it was one of the war years an' metal was scarce," says Casey, "so they never did get around to it."

Charley Grimm, as great a baseball buffoon as Casey, was running the Milwaukee club, then in the American Association, in partnership with Bill Veeck. Veeck went into military service and Grimm was asked to return as manager of the Chicago Cubs. Charley said he'd take the job if Casey, through in Boston, would take over Milwaukee for him.

Casey agreed and when the word reached Veeck on some South Pacific Island with the Marines, it had almost the same affect on him as shell-fire. He exploded in letters to Mickey Heath and other Milwaukee officials all season. He wrote, among other things, that he didn't like Stengel, thought him a poor manager, didn't think he fit in with plans for the future, was tight-fisted and couldn't evaluate ball players.

Stengel's answer to all this was to win the pennant by seven games. It was Casey's first championship club since his Toledo team won the Association flag in 1927. Later Veeck returned, met Stengel for the first time, saw that he had not only maintained the club's high attendance but sold a number of players to major league clubs. He offered Casey the job again but Casey had already resigned.

It was Stengel's idea to stay out of baseball and give the Texas oil wells another whirl in 1945, but George Weiss persuaded him to manage Kansas City, which was the Yankees' farm in the American Association at the time. The war had stripped the club of most of its quality players, so his seventh place finish wasn't held against him.

The years, not to mention the poor ball players, were beginning to tell on Stengel and he again thought of calling it a career. But back on the Coast, Brick Laws, one of the owners of the Oakland club, began to woo him. He finally won his man. The chance to spend more time in his Glendale home appealed to Casey and so did the long seven-game series in vogue in the league. He took the Oakland job, finished second in his first year, fourth the next season and then first.

The Yankees had lost the 1948 pennant under Bucky Harris and during the World Series they announced that Harris was being dropped. Speculation on his successor continued through the Series. Those who knew how close Weiss and Stengel had been for years, however, put their money on Casey. On October 12 it was announced that Stengel had been signed to a two-year contract.

Back in the early 1940s Joe McCarthy, then the Yankee manager, had developed a chronic stomach disorder which caused him to talk of quitting.

Ed Barrow, the general manager, talked to Weiss, then

his assistant in charge of the farm system about lining a man up just in case McCarthy decided to step down.

"I've got just the man you want," said George, "Casey Stengel."

Barrow snorted at the name. Stengel, he said, was only a clown.

Weiss persisted, waited his chance and, after the firing of Harris, brought Stengel in to fill the biggest, most lush job in baseball.

"If you weren't a baseball man you might think Stengel was crazy," Weiss said at the time, "But if you were, well, when you finally got to sleep—and the chances are he'd be sitting on the other bed and still talking—you would wake up discovering that you were really learning things.

"I suppose I have stayed up later and talked longer, or rather listened longer, with Casey than anybody else in baseball," says Weiss.

"I was convinced he was a great baseball man 25 years ago and I am now. He is all baseball, a man dedicated to the game. It pours out of him.

"He does things at times that surprise you. Like sending up three lefthanded pinch-hitters against a lefthanded pitcher for example. He doesn't hesitate to go against the book. But when you ask him about it he comes up with reasons so sound you find you're learning from him.

"He did something when he was managing in Boston that would have to impress any baseball man. The Braves couldn't be considered a good investment then, but Casey put some of his own money into the club. Not many would be willing to do that; they'd rather use somebody else's money.

"When he was managing Oakland we had two good scouts on the Coast, Joe Devine and Bill Essick. They both sent in favorable reports on him. Stengel, they told us, was the manager in that league."

"But Casey didn't get this job through friendship. The Yankees represent an investment of millions of dollars and don't give away jobs just because you're a good story teller. He got the job because the Yankees believed he could produce for· them."

His reception was a bit on the chilly side. Harris was well liked and his friends suspected that Stengel's selection was a plot to soften them up because of Casey's known popularity.

"I remember one of the first press conferences," Stengel says. "Somebody asked a question about Joe DiMaggio and I said I couldn't answer it then because I didn't know Joe DiMaggio. I knew his brother Vince DiMaggio because I had him in Boston. But I didn't know Joe and said so. I could hear the hum in the background. Then they asked questions about the pennant chances and I said I would have to wait until I saw my players for the first time at spring training an' I could hear that hum again an' knew what they were sayin'. They were sayin', 'Why this bum managed nine years an' never even got into the first division.' "

Dave Egan, an old critic of Casey's on the *Boston Record*, wound up his typewriter and let Stengel have it:

"The Yankees have now been mathematically eliminated from the 1949 pennant race. They eliminated themselves when they engaged Perfesser Casey Stengel to mismanage them for the next two years, and you may be sure that the Perfesser will oblige to the best of his unique ability."

In nine years as a manager in the National League Stengel had never been able to bring his team home higher than fifth place. In twelve out of 20 years in the minors, his teams finished in the second division. But, except for

Milwaukee, where he won the American Association pennant in 1944, this was the first time he had ever taken over an established first-division club. The Yankees had finished third behind Cleveland and Boston in 1948.

Now, in his first year as manager of the New York Yankees he won the American League pennant and the World Series. He was hailed as a genius. The Baseball Writers Association of America voted him the Manager of the Year and the New York members presented him with the appropriate hardware at their annual banquet.

Stengel met Billy Meyer, the manager of the Pittsburgh Pirates at the affair. Billy had been named Manager of the Year in 1948, but then had a miserable 1949.

"What I can't understand, Billy," Casey said to his old friend, "is how I suddenly got so smart and you got so dumb?"

Weiss's faith in Stengel had been justified.

Stengel was credited with starting the two-platoon system in 1949, his first Yankee year. Actually he had used it his last two years at Oakland.

It was more noticeable on the Yankees because he platooned great players, like Charley Keller and Tommy Henrich. He also platooned second baseman Snuffy Stirnweiss, who had once led the American League in hitting. Only Joe DiMaggio, when he was in good working order, Phil Rizzuto and Yogi Berra were fixtures.

"I had to platoon Henrich, who played first base an' the outfield for me because he had a bad knee that acted up at times," said Casey, "an' Keller had a bad back. When a player gets aged, if you rest him now and then he'll run better for five or so days an' swing a quicker bat.

"I alternated Cliff Mapes, Johnny Lindell, Gene Woodling an' Hank Bauer in the outfield. I'd rest Stirnweiss some an' play young Jerry Coleman at second, an' platoon Bobby Brown an' Billy Johnson at third.

"It made some of them mad they didn't get to play all the time but it didn't get me mad. An' after a while Bauer an' Woodling, who used to get the maddest when platooned, got to overcome what hittin' weaknesses they had at the start an' they became fine hitters an' had to play all the time.

"I never did stick to one lineup or battin' order with the Yankees an' I'll tell you why. The answer is that they weren't all Joe DiMaggios or Mickey Mantles. I platooned my players to get the most out of them, considerin' their age, condition an' how they went against certain types of pitchin'. I'd also think of the ball park we were playin' in. Like in Yankee Stadium I liked lefthanded hitters because of that short right field. An' if the other club started a pitcher I believed a good touch for lefthanded hitters I had them battin' second, third, fourth an' fifth.

"The way I moved players up an' down the battin' order bothered a lot of people but it never bothered me.

The two managers meet at home plate before a game to discuss ground rules and then present their lineup cards to the umpires. Often, when Casey clumped out he would pause after the other manager had given his lineup, and act like a man who had misplaced the shopping list his wife had given him. He'd reach into a rear pocket for a lineup card, start to hand it over and then pull it back with, "Nope, that ain't the right one."

Before a big game he might come to home plate with a full house of lineup cards in his pocket and go through a long routine before handing the last one over.

"I gotta be careful," he once said, "for anything I might hear or see at the last minute an' I gotta be ready for that other manager maybe switchin' pitchers or others on me. I gotta pocketful of lineups for anything he might try."

For twelve years, 1949 through 1961, Casey Stengel's Yankees were part of the World Series panorama ten times, an unparalleled record for near perfection. In 1954 they slipped to second and again in 1959, but they were top banana every other time out.

Casey set personal marks which demolished those set by John McGraw, Joe McCarthy, Miller Huggins and Connie Mack, baseball's most successful managers before he went to work in earnest with that good Yankee material.

In his 30 years with the old New York Giants McGraw won 10 National League championships and three World Series; in 50 years as manager of the Philadelphia Athletics Mack won nine American League championships and five World Series; in 15½ seasons under McCarthy, the Yanks won the American League championship eight times and won seven World Series; in 12 years with the Yanks, Huggins won six championships and three World Series.

Until he came bouncing back from the minors to make like a genius, only McGraw and McCarthy had won four league championships in a row. Stengel won five American League titles in succession.

Stengel once said that if the Yankees lost a World Championship he would quit baseball. In 1960 they lost it in the seventh game to the Pittsburgh Pirates, but he never had a chance to make up his mind about resigning. The Yankees did it for him.

"If we'd been a little luckier an' won that last World Series game from the Pirates I don't think it would have made any difference," he said afterwards. "They'd made up their minds an' explained it as puttin' a new program in which it said your time was up at sixty-five. The last month of that 1960 season I knew I was through because the attitude of the people in the front office, outside of Mr. Weiss, was different. It was as though they had heard the word.

"Then, after the Series I was asked to meet Dan Topping an' Del Webb at the Waldorf Astoria. I was pretty sure what was going to happen. There wasn't any contract on the table for me to sign. When you don't see that paper anywhere in sight you just know they're gonna' lower the boom on you."

People were shocked and saddened. The staid New York Times ran an editorial which said, in part:

CASEY THUMBED OUT AT 70

The New Yorker's heart is heavy with the departure of Casey Stengel . . . He doesn't have to be a baseball fan to feel the pathos of those last words, said at 70, "My services were no longer desired." After all, a baseball ownership wants a winner and Casey's team had only won ten American League pennants in twelve years with him in the dugout. Obviously the man wasn't consistent.

The Baseball Hall of Fame? Casey was in it long ago in the esteem of his countrymen. He is secure in a first place of affection for the pleasure he has given us all through these many years.

Once again the New York Chapter of the Baseball Writer's Association organized a banquet for Casey after a firing. It was held in the Waldorf Astoria's Starlight Roof just twenty-four hours after the press conference. All the sportswriters were there, plus Jim Farley, George Weiss (who was out shortly, too), Branch Rickey, Ford Frick, Jack Mara, Ned Irish, Joe Cronin, president of the American League, and Red Blaik, the former Army football coach. Also players Ed Lopat, Elston Howard, Bill Skowron and Gil McDougald. Whitey Ford sent a telegram saying," You know how I love parties, but this is one I wish was never held."

Stengel spoke in relays between the other speakers: "I don't want to put the ridicule on Mr. Topping who has the nerve an' guts to come here tonight. Up to November I'm still working for the Yankees an' I had to put the date in to get that $160,000 due me from their profit-sharin' plan. I want to say one final thing. Don't ever give up. Tomorrow is just another day an' that's myself."

Topping spoke briefly, uncomfortably, saying: "Maybe I should just shut up. I feel like Khrushchev entering the United Nations but I'm not going to take off my shoe."

Stengel's dismissal caused astonishment all over the country. Wrote Joe Barry, in his column in the Kentucky Irish-American, of the Yankees' adoption of a retirement age:

"Does this mean that when Yogi Berra reaches sixty-five, he has to stop catching?"

Thus Casey went home to Edna and Glendale. He went to other banquets, gave his life story to the *Saturday Evening Post* for $150,000, and puttered around the lovely home Edna's father had built for them. In December he became a stockholder and director of the Valley National Bank in Glendale.

He had been approached about managing Kansas City by a group that sought to buy that club even before he left the Yankees. After the season he received offers from the Detroit Tigers, the Los Angeles Angels and the new owners of the Washington Senators. He brushed them all off. But when George Weiss, representing the Mets, went after him as he had in the past, Casey was back in harness again.

He soon showed that he had lost none of his rare industry and wit, or ability to manage, rate ball players, teach the fundamentals and everything else about the game, tell stories in island-hopping fashion and stay up all night or thereabouts. This despite the fact that he was again dealing mostly with sad sack talent as in those basement-bent days in Brooklyn and Boston.

The days and nights were long, the travail terrible as the Mets lost and lost and lost. But always he was there, on the button, his seamed face serious or comic as the occasion demanded, his palm-leaf ears hearing everything, his wise old eyes everywhere and his brain working on all cylinders. When he wasn't pacing the dugout, you would see him there, one foot on the top step as though waiting for one of the many buglers in the stands to sound the call to charge.

SPRINGSVILLE

On February 19, 1962, the first group of players assembled on Miller Huggins Field in St. Petersburg and the Mets uniform was seen for the first time. Most of those who wore it were strangers to the citizens who turned out to watch this historic tableau but not the bandy-legged old gentleman with the figure 37 on the back of his shirt.

Casey Stengel, the man with the biggest ears, loudest voice and keenest sense of humor in baseball had been a regular visitor for many earlier years as manager of the Yankees and was as much an institution in the Sunshine City as the green benches, the shuffleboard courts and the Central Avenue booths that give blood pressure readings for 25 cents.

"You can do it, Case'," yelled the old folks who made up most of the audience, "Show 'em, Case'!"

"Oh Casey, autograph this for my husband will you?" asked a little old lady extending paper and pencil. "He's too bashful."

"What's his name?" Casey asked and wrote, "To my old pal Johnny White—Casey Stengel."

"Attaboy, Casey," "You tell 'em, Casey," came more shouts from the fans, many of them members of the Kids and Kubs, the old gaffers of 75 and over who play softball for the city's famous Three-Quarter-Century Club. Stengel winked at them, waved and then jogged out to the waiting group of players.

"Now this," he said, reaching into a back pocket for a ball, and holding it out for all to see, "is a baseball."

After he thought that fundamental had been grasped, he took them on a slow tour of the infield, kicking first base, then second and third and finally home, talking and gesticulating all the while. Finally he left them to the coaches and went to chat with some visiting Chicago journalists.

While talking to John Carmichael of the Chicago Daily News and Warren Brown of the Chicago American he noticed Jay Hook, a pitcher acquired from the Cincinnati Reds, off by himself in a corner of the field going through some strange physical gyrations with the aid of a rope. He left his visitors shortly and walked down to the pitcher.

Hook had been completing his course for a master's degree at Northwestern. During the football season he had watched the football coach giving special exercises to the squad.

"They were using a rope like this," Hook explained. "It's called an *isometric* rope, designed to get the maximum effort out of the muscle involved. You tug away at it for eight seconds or so, mainly to stretch thigh and back muscles. I remembered some of the things Otis Douglas, the Cincinnati trainer, had taught me. I just combined the two and came up with these exercises."

"I think you got somethin' there," said Casey. "If it can build muscles on football players it's good enough for my fellas. So suppose you get some more ropes an' start givin' them a drill out here before practice every morning."

And that's how the Mets acquired an athletic director.
George Weiss had wisely thought of St. Petersburg
months before accepting the Mets job. He knew that the
Yankees, who had trained there for three decades, were
moving to Fort Lauderdale on Florida's East Coast. He
also thought he might soon be back in the baseball business. He telephoned Elon C. "Robby" Robison, Chairman of the Florida Baseball Commission in St. Petersburg,
and asked him to save the facilities there for him, even
though he was still not back in the game.

The collection of admission dollars at spring exhibition
games is always important, of course, to help defray ex-
penses. St. Petersburg had, in a baseball sense, become a
New York town. In its exploding population were a lot
of New Yorkers who had either retired there or made it
their spot in the sun every winter. A solid segment of the
population is made up of retired New York City policemen, firemen and city workers. In the past they followed
the Yankees. Now they were solidly behind the Mets.

Stengel seemed more active in his first week of spring
training as manager of the Mets than he had ever seemed
in his days as boss of the Yankees. When he wasn't taking
groups of young players on a tour of the field, he was
spryly demonstrating base-running technique, or lecturing
them on hitting or fielding. He was all over the place,
watching a pitcher here or a second base combination
there, holding impromptu press conferences in the dugout, making radio and TV appearances and mugging for
the amateur movie makers.

Usually he'd be breakfasting in the dining room of the
Colonial Inn on St. Petersburg Beach before his players
were up. Then he'd drive his rented car to Miller Huggins
Field and be in his uniform before their bus arrived. Before the start of the exhibition schedule there would
usually be morning and afternoon practice sessions and

he'd still be there, talking to his coaches, reporters and visitors long after the players had left.

The exhibition games were held in Al Lang Field, on the downtown waterfront and when the games were over Casey would be available in a press room well stocked with drink and delicatessen foods in the nearby Soreno Hotel. He would talk for hours in the Soreno, particularly if out-of-town journalists, officials or old ball players were there, wearing out his scouts and many of the reporters. After a late dinner he would most likely be in the lounge of the club's hotel on the beach.

Once he announced that he was determined to go to bed at ten o'clock. It was the night before the Mets were to break camp and start the journey North. At ten, sure enough, he went to his room and retired. But he was up at three o'clock in the morning packing his trunk.

"Walked around until they opened for breakfast," he said. "Couldn't sleep any more."

"He works harder than any of us," says Kerby Farrell, the former Cleveland manager who was to handle the Mets Buffalo farm club in the International League after helping with the early training. "Seven days a week, harder and longer. He's the first one on the field in the morning and he's still there late in the afternoon. Then he'll talk all night. His energy is amazing."

Solly Hemus, one of the coaches, nods in agreement. "Its great to be associated with the old fellow after all these years. Only the other day Casey was saying, 'We don't want anybody to embarrass this club by not wanting to be a big leaguer,' and I agree. They shouldn't be here if they don't feel the urge. Casey wouldn't be taking over a make-shift operation and the players have confidence because they know that."

Stengel gathered his players around him for one early meeting in which he talked mostly about money and the opportunity of getting a lot of it as a member of the Mets. He meant, of course, Mrs. Payson's money. A listening newspaperman remarked that that was Whitney money, and Casey had a story for illustration.

"Alf Vanderbilt was driving through the gates of Belmont Park one day in one of those small cars," he said. "They passed Jock Whitney in a chauffer-driven foreign limousine. Vanderbilt, worth a fat pile himself, pointed to Jock and told Bill Winfrey, his trainer, 'Y'know if we had that fella's money we wouldn't have to work for a living.'

"Now this here club has a treee-mendous lot of money behind it," he told the assembled Mets, "an' while some of you young fellas may not be gettin' an awful lot of it right now, if you play the right kind of baseball for us those wallets will get fat as anything, an' someday you'll make some established big leaguers look like poor people if you cut the mustard."

Once Miller Huggins Field was known as Crescent Lake Park, and the spikes that punctured its turf were worn by Babe Ruth, Lou Gehrig, Bob Meusel and other Yankee greats.

Now, besides some name players a bit past their prime, the field was full of unknowns, reminding one of Branch Rickey's forecast when he was shilling for the ill-fated Continental League:

"The least of our worries will be finding players. They'll come down from the hills, from the plains and from the city streets for an opportunity to play."

Months before the camp opened, the New York office had been bombarded with letters from young and old ball players with semi-pro, college or high school experience—or less—asking for a try-out in St. Petersburg. Late letters of application awaited the Mets in Florida. And then there were the hopefuls there to apply in person.

One such applicant was John Papas, a 21-year clerk from Astoria, Long Island, who flew down from New York on a night coach jet. Arriving at six o'clock in the morning he told the sleepy clerk at the Colonial Inn he was trying out for the team and got a room at the baseball rate. He had some $200 left, enough he figured, for a two-week try.

He approached Johnny Murphy, Weiss's assistant, at the park next morning and said he was after a job. A dark, slim youngster about 5' 10", he wore cuffless trousers, a gold tie and pointed Italian shoes. Murphy thought he was applying for a job as clubhouse boy.

"No, I'm a ball player," he said, "a pitcher. I played in the Police Athletic League. I'm in good shape, I've been running nights."

"How could you work out in New York?" somebody said, "it's been snowing hard there."

"Yeah, but it was dry under the Tri-Borough Bridge," he said. "No snow there. I threw balls against the side wall of the bridge. People who saw me thought I was nuts, but I didn't care."

"You mean to say you came all the way down here without even writing us?" asked Murphy.

"I asked for a try-out last summer," the boy explained, "but never got an answer."

"Well, we can't give you any time here," said Murphy. "But if you can find somebody who'll catch for you on some field here I'll look at you. If we took everybody who came into camp like you we'd have 6,000 kids here."

One night all of Casey Stengel's guests except Coach Red Kress and a few newspapermen had left his suite in the Colonial Inn when the telephone rang.

"Hello, this is Ace Haggerty," said a voice. "You're a lucky manager. I coulda reported to some other club but I picked you."

"Who are you?" asked Casey.

"Ace Haggerty, 'the complete ball player,'" was the answer. "I'll be at your door in a few minutes."

Mr. Haggerty was as good as his threat. He proved to be a big balding man in his early forties, and he held a baseball in each fist.

"I pitch mostly, and with either arm," he announced, "an' I can also play the infield, the outfield an' catch. I'm one of the strongest men in the country. Here, try an' take the baseball out of either my hands. Just try it."

The Ace held his fists out to Casey but the manager passed up the invitation.

"You better sign me right up an' start seein' where you can use me tomorrow," said Haggerty. "I've come all the way from St. Louis."

"Nobody asked you, least ways I didn't," said Casey. "I should think you'd wait to be asked before travelin' all the way from St. Louis."

"You'd have invited me but you didn't know me," said Mr. Haggerty. "I been outa' baseball ten years workin' as an undertaker's assistant. But I played nights on the sandlots an' found out I was better than when I was a youngster. I got more strength in my wrists. Here, try an' take one of these baseballs away from me.

"I gotta ten thousand dollar bonus offer from another club in Florida, but I turned it down," said Mr. Haggerty. "I'd rather be with the Mets; I always wanted to see New York."

"I have to say I'm sorry I can't sign you," said Casey. "You see my owners wouldn't like it if I had a pitcher who pitched with both arms. They'd say I was a screwball or somethin'. So why don't you go over to Sarasota an' talk to Mr. Al Lopez, the manager of the Chicago White Sox. He's an old catcher an' likes all kinds of pitchers."

Mr. Haggerty lingered a few moments longer, then decided to depart. Halfway out the door he turned to tell

Stengel he'd be sorry when he came back with the Phillies or some other club and pitched a no-hitter against the Mets.

"An' I didn't see you try an' take those baseballs outa' my hands, either," was his parting shot.

Stengel closed the door on Mr. Haggerty, then winked and said that a manager had to be careful about recommending strange pitchers to other managers, and he hoped the fellow would forget about visiting Lopez.

"I had a pitcher when I managed Toledo," Casey suddenly recalled, "who had the strangest windup you ever saw—practically no windup at all. He said it happened that way because he lived in the Bronx an' his mother thought the streets were dangerous an' wouldn't let him outside to play. So he learned to pitch in the hallway of his apartment house, a very narrow hallway.

"He won some games for me, but at the end of the season we were doin' so bad I had to let him go. Then next spring I get a letter from him sayin' his arm was great again an' since he lived in New York would I recommend him to the Giants.

"I did, an' his first day in the Polo Grounds they let him pitch battin' practice. He broke a guy's arm with the first pitch. They run him outa' there fast an' McGraw gave me hell for recommendin' him."

On one side of Miller Huggins Field were two personalized benches. One painted green had "George Weiss" on it. The bench beside it was painted cream and was stenciled "Casey Stengel." Flaunting authority, Stengel would sit on "George Weiss" and hold press conferences.

"You want me to talk about my team," he began one day, "an' none of my New York writers is here. How long you gonna' be in town?"

"Just a few days," said Furman Bisher, of the Atlanta Journal, "but we reserved this day just for you."

"Well," he said, "I suppose you want to know how this ball club is gonna' be run an' I say I don't know because it's never been run before.

"Now you start with the catchin' an you got Coleman. He is a pull hitter an' fast on his feet an' very excellent in pickin' up low pitches. The question is, can he hit? Then there is 'Canzoneri' [*actually Chris Cannizzaro, but Casey always gives him the prize-fighter's tag*]. He's an exceptional thrower an', in justice to him, he took off ten pounds. Then Landrith an' Ginzberg have big-league alertness.

"Now about the infield, Hodges is seriously tryin' to improve his batting with help from Mr. Hornsby. Some of the plays he makes in the field saves you two, three runs. He saves a pitcher 30, 40 hits a year, maybe 60.

"If we go to Neal at second base in some games, I must say, he can be phenomenal. He makes mistakes on fly balls over his head but not on grounders. He's got some good points at the plate. When the ball goes, it's not a pop fly.

"First I thought Chacon could play short but he's hurt now, an' maybe it's Mantilla instead, an' when Chacon comes back I might escort him out to centerfield where he can also play because he can catch up with a ball very good.

"In the outfield we started with three experienced men, an' the man in right field can hit lefthanders better than righthanders. If they don't cover enough ground it will affect my pitchin' an I'll use the other men.

"You ask me about my pitchin' an I say that's the most important part of the ball club. I got some with big league ability who should be able to go five innings, an' some maybe more, an' some who got points as relief men. Some are very eager young men an' some had fair years on bad ball clubs. Then there are some who look excellent in their new uniforms when the photographers ask them to pose but the question is what will they look like when those big, mean batters step up to the plate? So I gotta' wait a little longer an' find out about *them*."

"Casey, you forgot about third base," said Ernie Mehl, of the Kansas City Star. "Who'll play there?"

"I'm glad you asked that question," he replied. "Now you take that fella who. . ."

On March 9, 1962, the Mets took the field for the first time to play another ball club and lost to the St. Louis Cardinals, 8-0. Jay Hook was the starting pitcher—and loser.

The days went by and no Met seemed capable of hitting a ball over the outfield fences in either batting practice or intra-squad games. The closest had been a blast by Bruce Fitzpatrick, a 19-year-old bonus shortstop from Springfield, Mass., that hit the base of the right field screen 440 feet from the plate during one bright morning's hitting re-hearsal.

The day following their first game, however, the Mets played the Cardinals again. They were losing 3-2 in the eighth when Choo Choo Coleman stepped up to the plate as a pinch-hitter and tied up the game with the club's first homer. Next inning they won for the first time, 4-3, as Elio Chacon slapped a single past third, allowing Richie Ashburn, who had doubled, to score standing up.

On March 22 came the game St. Petersburg had been waiting for—the first meeting of the Yankees and the Mets.

When Casey Stengel entered Al Lang Field the applause began as soon as the crowd spotted him in the passageway leading toward the dugout. He shoved past a few auto-graph-seekers until he was directly in front of the Yankee dugout and stopped there to sign a baseball for a boy.

Ralph Houk, who had succeeded him as manager saw

Casey then, his back toward the bench and no Yankee near him. He jumped to his feet and ran out. He had to touch Stengel from behind before his old boss turned. Then they shook hands. They repeated the act for the cameramen but none of the photographs would show the instant of strain for both men in that first handshake.

A reporter with Stengel said, "Hey Case', your old assistant manager here wants to give you some advice."

Stengel turned quickly and grinned. It was Yogi Berra. More pictures, then, with Berra, Mickey Mantle, Roger Maris, Johnny Sain and Frank Crosetti. The last two had been his coaches. The applause followed him wherever he went.

Berra stood on the side now, watching and listening. Beside him a friend, caught up in the fever of the occasion, said, "That Stengel! Just listen to the people cheering him!"

"I just hope," answered Yogi, "that it keeps up."

After he'd met Mantle and Maris, Casey said, "I wish you guys both a lotta' luck, but just hit grounders today."

Then his Mets went on to beat the Yankees, 4–3, before 6,000 customers who sounded mighty pleased. They won it in the ninth when Casey sent Richie Ashburn up to pinch-hit and the man did what he was told—lined a single to right.

They won some and they lost some, and finally they broke camp and headed for New York for better or for worse. At Portsmouth, Va., they stopped for an exhibition game scheduled with the Baltimore Orioles, but rain had made the field unfit for baseball.

Stengel "played," however, speaking before 450 men, women and children attending a unity breakfast at nine o'clock in the morning. He talked about his pitchers, catchers, infielders, coaches and even the broadcasters, but didn't mention any of his outfielders.

"I didn't give their names," he told someone in confidence afterwards, "because while we're goin' home with eight men hittin' .200 or less, my outfielders have done better. In fact, I got one who must be hittin' .600, an' I don't want some club to catch up with us an' try an' get him."

Scar tissue from those 120 beatings in their first frightful season had disappeared when the Mets assembled for better or for worse on the same St. Petersburg rehearsal grounds in March of 1963 to get in shape for their second season. The sun shone, the birds sang and the senior citizens of that geriatric town again swarmed to watch them.

Something new had been added. Outside the field stood a man hawking single-sheet programs.

"Names and numbers of all the Mets, new and old," he shouted. "Meet the Mets—the next baseball champeens of the world!"

There was some early holdout trouble. Marv Throneberry hadn't signed a contract but he reported to St. Petersburg to talk terms. Gene Woodling, who had served as player representative on other clubs and who had come to camp this time as a player-coach, decided to speak for Throneberry when it appeared that no contract talks would develop. In the opinion of the club he talked a little too harshly in public to Johnny Murphy on Marv's behalf. So it was decided that Woodling would be made a free agent, even though this meant losing one of the Mets' few established hitters. Then, Throneberry agreed to terms.

"When you were talking contract," somebody asked, "didn't you mention the fact that you brought some people into the park last summer?"

"Sure," he said, "and they told me that I also chased some away."

It appeared early in rehearsal that there wouldn't be much change in the cast, though only 16 of the 46 men

were holdovers! The only new members who looked as
though they might make the opening-day lineup were
second baseman Ron Hunt, third baseman Pumpsie
Green, first baseman Tim Harkness and Outfielder Dick
Smith. Harkness had been obtained from the Dodgers in
a winter trade for pitcher Bob Miller, Green had been
obtained from the Boston Red Sox, along with shortstop
Al Moran and pitcher Tracey Stallard, for infielder Felix
Mantilla.

The rest of the roster included such familiar names as
catcher Choo Choo Coleman, infielders Charley Neal,
Elio Chacon and Gil Hodges, outfielders Jim Hickman
and Joe Christopher and pitchers Roger Craig, Jay Hook,
Al Jackson, Craig Anderson and Ken McKenzie.

Hodges, who had undergone an operation for the re-
moval of cartilage from his left knee during the winter,
was moving cautiously. Harkness couldn't run because of a
pulled leg muscle. Chris Cannizzaro had a busted finger
and Catcher Norm Sherry a cantaloup on his skull where
Bob Cerv's bat had landed accidentally. All told, 16 patients were awaiting Dr. Peter La Motte, the club physi-
cian, when he arrived from New York.

There was something wrong with Neal too, his innards.
The doctor was asked about Neal's trouble.

"Nothing serious," he said. "Gastro-enteritis. In un-
orthodox medical terms, the crud."

Just how far the Mets had come under the baton of
Casey Stengel was illustrated one day toward the close of
the club's second spring training stay.

Club officials were approached by the management of
Madame Josephine Tussaud's London Wax Museum, a
branch of which had opened at St. Petersburg Beach not
far from where the Mets themselves were on exhibition
at feeding and leisure time. It seems the museum already

had a wax likeness of Stan Musial, the great Cardinal star, and now they were considering adding the figures of Casey Stengel and some of his players.

"I beg your pardon," said their representative to Stengel, "but I'm from London and . . ."

"You want me to tell you about my ball club, I suppose," said Casey, thinking he was talking to another visiting journalist. "Well my owners may not want me to talk to any foreign papers because we don't plan to play any games in England just yet," he rushed on, "but a fella you know named the Duke of Windsor talked to me in my dugout when I was managin' the Yankees, an' we just bought a fella named Duke Snider from Los Angeles to play right field, which is over there by that big water tower and . . ."

Half an hour later the stranger had a complete rundown on what "fellas" Stengel might play if he didn't play some others in their places. The man from London went back to his museum and sat among the wax works until his head had cleared.

Later they lured Casey to the museum so that he could see what company he and his players would be in. They showed him the President and Mrs. Kennedy, Winston Churchill, Princess Grace and Prince Rainier of Monaco, Nikita Khrushchev and Elvis Presley. Then they led him to the figure of Musial.

"Jus' let me stand here a while," he said. "It's probably the only chance I'll get to watch this fella for five minutes without seein' him bust up a ball game on me."

Among the Met figures mentioned as likely to join Stengel in the sports wing of the museum were Gil Hodges, Cookie Lavagetto, Frank Thomas, Choo Choo Coleman, Mrs. Joan Payson, George Weiss and, of course, Marvelous Marv Throneberry.

"But first," said Stengel cautiously, "my owners'll probably want it in writin' that they won't put any of my players in what you call your Chamber of Horrors."

During the early intra-squad game days, Stengel found himself a little short of outfielders. Richie Ashburn had retired, Gene Woodling had been given his release and Frank Thomas was holding out for a fatter contract.

Casey put Charley Neal, the infielder, in right field for one six-inning game, and Neal promptly threw out three swifties who thought they would be able to run on him.

Neal then turned toward Stengel, who used to play some right field himself, and said with a straightface, "Nothing to playing this position, nothing at all."

Before they left camp the Mets had won the first title of their existence—the championship of the city of St. Petersburg. They beat the St. Louis Cardinals, who also train there, 6–2, on April 2, in the deciding game of a series. They did it with a five-run rally in the eighth inning after being held to just two hits through the first seven frames.

THAT FIRST HORRENDOUS SEASON

The Mets had finished their first spring with an exhibition game record of 12 victories and 12 defeats.

"We had a remarkable spring record for the kind of club they say we are," Casey Stengel declared on arrival in New York. "But the record don't fool me. I *think* I'm gonna' win every day, sure, an' I'm mad if I don't win. But I know in a lotta' games if the other side put in their regulars we wouldna' beaten 'em at all."

Casey, Weiss and the players rode up lower Broadway in open cars on April 12, the day before their home opener, as the ticker-tape, torn newspapers and an occasional complete telephone book rained down upon them. It was one of the few parades to a City Hall reception in which the lunch-time office workers crowding the sidewalks to watch didn't turn to one another and say:

"What's this one all about? The old geezer wavin' his hat in the first car—who's he?"

"Everybody receives us wonderful," Casey had said. "The public thinks we can beat anybody. It's amazin'."

From the City Hall Stengel and his players went to the

57

Polo Grounds where they had their last workout before the start of the season.

Freshly-painted signs along the outfield walls greeted them.

"By golly, look at that will you?" exclaimed Marv Throneberry, pointing to one of the larger ads, "Fifty thousand dollars if you hit that sign!"

"Not fifty thousand dollars, you dope," said Rod Kanehl, "fifty thousand trading stamps."

Richie Ashburn, the singles hitter, looked at the close upper stands fondly.

"Boy it's good to be back," he said. "This is where I hit twenty-five per cent of my home runs."

It was true. Eleven years ago as a member of the Phillies he had hit a total of four home runs. One of them was hit at the Polo Grounds.

In the ancient clubhouse, with its leaking pipes and sagging floors, they found Herb Norman, the equipment manager, and his assistant Frank Prudenti, unwrapping the stylish royal blue blazers with Mets insignia on the breast.

"You're supposed to wear these as much as you can," said Herb, "so you'll look good and identify yourselves with the team, particularly on the road. You put one arm in a sleeve at a time, just like this, see?"

On April 11, 1962, in the city of St. Louis, the newly-minted Mets were asked to expose themselves to the paying public in a National League game for the first time. Here they got one of the few breaks they were to get all season. It rained and the game was postponed.

The next night was clear, however, and the game was a romp for the Cardinals. They won, 11–4, with Larry Jackson pitching. Roger Craig started for the Mets and when he made a balk with a runner on third in the first inning, the Mets found themselves behind, 1–0, with their first game just six minutes old.

In their first batting order were Ashburn, cf; Mantilla, ss; Neal, 2b; Thomas, lf; Bell, rf; Hodges, 1b; Zimmer, 3b; Landrith, c, and Craig, p. Before the game ended two hours and 53 minutes after its start, Bob Moorehead, Herb Moford and Clem Labine had been used as relief pitchers and Ed Bouchee and Jim Marshall had been asked to pinch-hit.

Gil Hodges hit the first home run for the Mets and Charley Neal hit another later, but there were few other bright moments for the new club. They made three errors, Landrith had three bases stolen on him without a throw coming close to an out, and there were many bad plays.

Even Hodges had an awful time. With a man on first base, Bill White hit a grounder past him. A few seasons back he would have used it to start a double-play. And in failing to cover when Craig tried to pick Stan Musial off first base, Gil shared in the blame for the pitcher's balk.

A dugout visitor had been afraid for them before the game even started. As they warmed up before batting practice, Thomas dropped his glove at his feet and yelled to Don Zimmer. Zimmer nodded like a man accepting a challenge, backed up about 60 feet and then fired. Thomas caught the ball with his two hands and didn't even shake them.

"Those guys playing catch bare-handed," the visitor said to Casey Stengel. "You'll have cripples before they throw out the first ball."

One who had been around explained that Thomas prided himself on his ability to catch anyone in the majors over the standard pitching distance bare-handed. He'd do it for money or fun. Once he had taken $10 from Willie Mays, who walked away rubbing his throwing arm.

"I do it lots of times," Thomas said when he came into the dugout. "It doesn't even sting. I'd be better off in the outfield without a glove, I guess, wouldn't I Zim?"

"I wouldn't bet against your going out there and trying it," answered Zimmer.

It hadn't been many seasons back when Zimmer, then with the Dodgers, had hung out of a tenth floor window of the Conrad Hilton Hotel in Chicago with his roomie, pitcher Ed Roebuck, holding his feet. There was a reason. Rube Walker, the reserve Brooklyn catcher, had remarked earlier that he was going to enjoy a room service dinner. "Big steak medium-rare," he said, "some hash-browns, a salad. And if they had any, one of those delicious chocolate éclairs."

Walker had the room beneath Zimmer and Roebuck. They called room service that evening to send up an éclair. It was simple then for Zimmer, with Roebuck's help, to deliver it. Swaying only slightly upside down above Michigan Boulevard, he made a good, strong throw and the éclair hit Walker, sitting at his dinner, right in the kisser.

The day after their sorry start in St. Louis was dark, dismal, drizzling and autumn-cold. It was also Friday the thirteenth, so naturally the Mets played their opening game at the Polo Grounds. Naturally too, they lost it to the Pittsburgh Pirates, 4–3.

The outfield was mud pudding, and players on both sides slipped, skidded and fell all through the game. One of the few bright spots in the park was the shocking pink bonnet worn by Mrs. Payson in the royal box.

Mayor Wagner showed up to throw out the first ball and was loudly booed, possibly by fans who blamed him for the failure to stop the Giants and Dodgers from moving West. M. Donald Grant, the chairman of the board, welcomed the shivering customers and suggested that they buy the iced beer of the Mets' television and radio sponsor.

The Pirates scored their first run because Ashburn and Bell let a catchable fly ball fall between them with a man on third and two out. Wild pitches helped Pittsburgh

score two more runs. Then Ray Daviault, pitching in relief in the eighth, wild-pitched Dick Groat across the plate.
Very sad.

"Maybe he should be a starter instead of a reliever,"
mused Stengel afterwards "although he is 29 years old an'
has been a reliever an' it is hard to change a man's life for
him. But I notice when he hasn't got anybody on base he
pitches low like he should an' when you are a relief pitcher
you are always comin' in with men on base. Also you remember this is his first big-league game an' he comes from
a nice family an' he never had the chance to make the big
dollar before."

Few of the 12,000 customers who attended seemed un-
duly disturbed over the unseemly outcome of the game.
The cheers for the Mets were as vociferous before the last
putout as they had been when the players were first introduced.

The shouts that greeted Gil Hodges's name when the
starting lineup was announced exceeded in volume and
duration even those for Casey Stengel, indicating that
many old Brooklyn customers were in the park. At the
time of the announcement it was not known that Hodges
would not play because of a strained leg muscle, so when
Jim Marshall was sent out to play first base instead the
people voiced much displeasure. Then when the correc-
tion was given over the public address system they began
to chorus, "We Want Hodges!" continuing the demand
throughout the game. In fact, when Marshall hit a two-
bagger to start an inning in which the Mets made their
first run, the cries became even more persistent.

Ball games weren't the only things lost. Before the season was many days old, in fact, Casey Stengel had lost $250.
That was the amount of the fine plastered on him by Commissioner of Baseball Ford Frick for posing in a beer ad
with Miss Rheingold while wearing his Mets uniform.

The ads, on big billboards on buildings and highways all over the metropolitan New York area, however, were in good taste. They did not suggest that Stengel—or even Miss Rheingold—drank beer. They merely proclaimed the relationship between ball club and the brewery sponsoring its telecasts and broadcasts.

The Mets were convinced that the fellow who blew the whistle to Frick came from the Madison Avenue agency of a disappointed beer sponsor.

Commissioner Frick said Casey's mistake was in wearing a Mets uniform. In point of fact it was an old Yankee uniform that they had put on Gary Cooper when he played the part of Lou Gehrig in the Hollywood movie, "Pride of the Yankees"—and thereby hangs a touching tale.

The agency people had sent Miss Rheingold and a crew of photographers, technicians, directors and make-up men out to Stengel's home in Glendale, California, to work up a spread of pictures for the planned newspaper and billboard advertisements before Casey went to Florida for spring training.

"He kept the uniform on after they'd all left the house," recalled Edna Stengel. "When it came time for dinner he arrived at the table still wearing the suit with the word METS scrawled in orange and blue script across the front. Later in the evening, when I happened to go into his den, there was Casey sprawled out with a book in his favorite arm-chair sound asleep still wearing the uniform. He did everything but wear it to bed instead of his pajamas—that's how glad he was to be in a baseball suit again."

Something happened to the Mets on the night of April 23 in Pittsburgh, something new and wonderful. They won their first game. They scored two runs in the very first inning off Tom Sturdivant, who had beaten them in New York. They batted around against Sturdivant and

Diomedes Olivo in the second. Elio Chacon, the dynamic shortstop, got three of their 14 hits. The score was 9 to 1, and there were 16,000 witnesses, most of them screaming Pittsburgh ladies, since it was the Pirates' first Ladies Night of the season.

The hero of the big win was Jay Hook, the 25-year-old righthander from Grayslake, Ill., who was a $125,000 premium purchase from the Cincinnati Reds in the player pool the previous October.

Hook pitched nine innings, held the Pirates to five hits, issued only one base on balls and hit a two-run single with three on base and none out in the second inning that raised the score to a comfortable 4–0 in his favor.

A member of the American Rocket Society, Hook got his master's degree in mechanical engineering from Northwestern University. His speciality was gas dynamics, the study, as he puts it, "of high speed air or gas flowing over a body or through a rocket nozzle."

An all-around athlete, he played basketball with some distinction at Northwestern. He looked so promising as a baseball pitcher that the Cincinnati Reds asked him to please take $50,000 in bonus money upon his graduation in 1957.

Unfortunately, Hook came from the Reds with a higher ratio of homers for innings pitched than any pitcher in the major leagues, which might have been one reason why they let him go. He had little fear of being damaged beyond repair by the Bucs this particular night, however, since he owned a fat 6–0 lead at the end of the second inning and could dare them to swing away.

A horde of photographers descended on the Mets' clubhouse in Forbes Field after he had retired the last Pittsburgh batter successfully. They shouted but not any louder than Stengel, who was sitting on a stool exactly where they had snapped him as the losing Yankee manager after the seventh and final game of the 1960 World Series.

"Don't take my picture," he yelled, "Take the picture of the boy that wins one. Come back an' see me when we win 26 straight."

It was a night for clowning and Stengel went on to say he'd probably make Hook the starting pitcher in the Mets' next 100 games.

"He has as much stuff as any pitcher in baseball," went on the manager, "but he won't brush them back. If he pitched like Sal Maglie nobody would beat him."

After their losing start the Mets went on to lose a record 140 games, while winning only 40. They had a terrible time putting victories together but losses were something else again. They managed to fashion a nine-game losing streak to open the season. Later they had a seven-game streak, then one of 11. Their biggest was a 17-game streak that included seven games lost by one run, a sure sign of a bad, bad ball club.

This dismal debacle began with a 3-2 defeat in Houston on May 21 and ended with a 2-1 loss in Philadelphia on June 6. At the early-morning post-mortem following the 10-1 demolishment by the Giants in San Francisco, Ed Sinclair, of the New York Herald Tribune, asked Stengel if he had thought of turning his athletes loose on the town some night.

"Nothing else seems to work," Eddie said. "And I remember hearing that you used to try and help the boys snap out of a slump that way when you were managing in Brooklyn. They got good saloons here. Maybe Lefty O'Doul would let them have a back room and their own bartender."

"No, I wouldn't want to try that remedy just yet," said Casey. "They'd be a risk because when they do things they do things very big—like this losin' streak. If I gave them the green light they might go out an' get to feelin' so sorry for themselves they'd drink the town dry an' then what would the public think of them, all strangers comin' in an' doin' that? I told them how I stood on drinking down in spring training."

Listeners were reminded of the evening in St. Petersburg that Stengel expressed his views. He started off by saying he had told the Mets he didn't mind them wetting their whistles after their baseball chores, providing they didn't do it by the numbers.

As a consequence, all turned out to be sweetness and light in St. Petersburg as far as the social behavior of the Mets were concerned. Only the senior citizens of the shuffleboard set had comparable records for sobriety, regular sack time and general goodness.

Not once did a Met wind up in the St. Pete pokey on charges of trying to climb a telephone pole at four o'clock in the morning or moon-bathing in Mirror Lake in the center of the city or wrestling a bartender for one-for-the-road.

"We haven't witnessed such exemplary behavior since the temperance people had a convention here last November," said hotelman Bud Smith, of the Soreno. "In fact, people are asking, are the Mets training for the new baseball season or the Peace Corps?"

The Mets lost nine of their first 11 games at the Polo Grounds, leading some to demand that the place be declared a disaster area. Then they got out of town and suddenly began to show muscle, skill and more runs than the other fellows on the scoreboard. In Philadelphia they ended one of their baby losing streaks, a five-gamer, with a 7–5 win. Then they flew to Chicago and beat the Cubs 3–1 on a four-hitter by Jay Hook for possession of ninth place.

"Must be no more'n a dozen fans up in those stands," said Casey Stengel, in Wrigley Field for the first time since he managed the Boston Braves in 1943. "Must be the cold weather. Couldn't be because they're playin' us."

Back at the Polo Grounds they delighted the faithful by splitting a four-game series with Milwaukee. Then they were off for Chicago again, where they won a double-header. On to Milwaukee now where the Braves called a halt to their giddy gait with a 5–2 decision.

That was the only game the Braves won in the series. The Mets won the next one, 6–5, and then swept a Sunday double-header, 7–6 and 9–6.

Sudsville was shocked, not only by the loss of three in a row to Casey's collection of culls and retreads but also by what Frank Thomas, whom the Braves had sold to the Mets, did to them. He had a hot hand in all three New York wins. He had eight hits in 18 times at bat for a total of 21 bases in the four-game series, with three homers, a triple and two doubles. He drove in seven runs and played left field better than Howie Bedell and Tommy Aaron, his rookie replacements.

Two other discards embarassed the Braves. Ken McKenzie, Stengel's "Yale fella," who had been a Milwaukee bullpen jobber, won both Saturday's game and the first one Sunday for his first two major league victories. And Felix Mantilla, whom they traded as a no-hit shortstop, hit a three-run homer in the Mets' six-run seventh inning of the second game.

They had won nine out of 12 games now, and there was much brave talk of the future. It faded fast. In Houston, the next stop, they lost 3–2 and were off on a miserable 17-game losing streak. They had taken ninth place from the Cubs during their spree, but three days after the Houston loss they were back in the basement again, destined to stay there for the rest of the season.

Thomas kept hitting homers—he finished with 34, one shy of his total with the Pittsburgh Pirates in 1958, his best home run year. He didn't, however, find the Polo Grounds the happy hunting ground he expected. His critics had another beef. He was the year's homer king with the bases empty, 25 of his 35 coming with them bare.

He was a lifetime, paid-up member of the pull-hitter's union and his strict adherence to the rules of the lodge sometimes made the manager fume.

One afternoon at the Polo Grounds Thomas was the batter in a situation that clearly called for hitting behind the runner on first base. Thomas had been hitting down the left field foul line and this time was no exception. He hit a one-bounce grounder to the third baseman, who started a double-play.

"If you want to be a sailor," yelled Stengel, "go join the Navy!"

This stumped the students of Stengelese in the dugout for a while. Finally they figured it out. Thomas, in Stengel's book, was trying to pull the ball instead of hitting to the opposite field, because he wanted to hit the circle on the clothing sign in left field and thus get some points toward the luxury motor cruiser offered as a prize.

One time in the middle of a 17-game losing streak Stengel sat on the bench watching the San Francisco Giants take their batting practice.

"Now which of my plumbers will I put in the lineup today?" he asked of no one in particular as he fingered the lineup card.

Charley Hoff, the pixyish sports photographer of the New York Daily News, and Tony Bernato, then on the New York Mirror, were sitting nearby.

"We'll fix a lineup for you, Casey," said Hoff, and took the card. He and Bernato held a meeting, filled out the card and returned it to Stengel shortly before the game was to start.

The four umpires and Giant manager Alvin Dark were

already assembled at home plate when Stengel trotted out. He dug in his back pocket and handed chief umpire, Tom Gorman his card. It listed nine strange names of nine news photographers who were covering the game.

"What's this?" asked Gorman, reading the lineup. "Where did these Mets come from? You bring a bunch down from Buffalo all of a sudden?"

Casey grabbed the card back and handed over the real one.

Majestically, like an old-line football coach seeking to inspire the lads to win one for the pretzel baron who paid most of their salaries, Casey Stengel turned to his Mets in the dugout before they went out to meet the Cardinals one night at the Polo Grounds and had this to say:

"She's just back from Europe where she's been hearin' bad things about us." He nodded to where Mrs. Payson was sitting in the royal box listening to M. Donald Grant, the chairman of the board, explaining why her lads had lost nine of their last 11 games and were a solid tenth, 31 games behind the leaders on July 6.

"Let's win one for the old girl!" he concluded with a shout.

The Mets, dutifully went out there and clobbered the Cards, 10 to 3. Mrs. Payson, who had never seen them win before, laughed and shouted in her happiness.

It was their first win over the Cards in four meetings. Gil Hodges hit his 370th homer, making him tenth on the list of career home-run hitters and first among the right-handed National League homer hitters. Rod Kanehl, a late-inning defensive replacement for Frank Thomas, hit his own and the Mets' first grand slammer during their six-run eighth inning.

Often after that, when the enemy had to be held off by the best defensive forces possible in the late innings, or when a pinch base-runner was needed, or a pinch-hitter, a sign or two might be hoisted by the fans in the stands facing the Mets dugout, instructing Casey to:

"Send in Kanehl."

Kanehl was a Met only because Stengel has a long memory. A veteran of eight years in the Yankee organization, all of them on league farm clubs, his name came up in the minor league draft and it rang a bell with Casey.

"I remembered him," said the manager. "He climbed a fence for me once."

What Casey remembered was an incident in the Yankees' pre-training camp instructional school in 1954, which Kanehl attended along with such Yankee rookies as Bobby Richardson, Jack Reed and Tony Kubek.

Once, during an inter-squad game, he had vaulted the fence, caught a long, high fly ball and jumped back over the fence again, all with the nonchalance of a fellow getting on and off a bicycle. The memory stayed with Stengel —like that one of watching Babe Herman of the old Dodgers catching the rebound of a fly ball off his own skull.

Sent up to pinch-hit with the bases loaded in a game with the Cincinnati Reds, Kanehl took a pitch on the fleshy part of his arm. When he reached first base, Rod patted his left sleeve, then motioned to the dugout. Trainer Gus Mauch, believing he was hurt, came running out.

Kanehl wasn't hurt, it developed. He simply wanted to remind the manager of the $50 bonus he had promised any player who got hit by a pitched ball in such a situation.

"Frank Crossetti used to lead the league in that play when he was the Yankee shortstop," recalled Casey, "an' before that you'd see Hughie Jennings do it a lot. But you can hardly get those kinda' players any more."

Kanehl was one of the happier Mets after their exhibition win over the Yankees at the Stadium.

"When Tom Greenwade, the scout, signed me for the Yankee organization years before," he recalled, "he told me I'd reach the Stadium some day and be with the winning team. I'll have to send him a telegram saying that he was right."

The Mets won a 9–8 ball game from the Cardinals in St. Louis on July 28, with Gene Woodling hitting a two-run homer and Craig Anderson saving it for Ken McKenzie with some tidy relief jobbing. The date was also memorable because it was the occasion of a party to celebrate Casey Stengel's 72nd birthday. At the Chase Hotel, a private party room was stocked with food, drink and chairs for listeners. They began listening early and were still at it when the cleaners went to work on the lobby floor in the early hours of the following morning.

He talked about the Mets, the size of the mosquitoes in the Houston ball park, bowling, his nieces and nephews, a Brooklyn undertaker named Mike Smith who used to take Western trips with the Dodgers for kicks.

He demonstrated Minnie Minoso's batting stance, Roger Craig's pick-off move to first base, and the way Umpire Bill Klem used to call strikes. He got down flat on the floor to show how Sherm Lollar, of the Chicago White Sox caught those low-ball pitchers and illustrated how Jerry Coleman made that cross-body throw at second base for a double-play.

"He was amazing, the way he did it," said Casey. "He'd throw the ball overhand, like this. He would throw it right there where he was lookin' without lookin' at it. He would throw the ball while he was in the air!"

He talked of his youth in Kansas City, and about Tom Prendergast, the political boss, who was "kind to the widow women."

Although he was only absent from his job a total of two days his first two seasons with the Mets, with the Yankees

Casey had been on sick call a number of times. Once in his last season he had suffered a severe virus attack and wound up in Lenox Hill Hospital. Visitors found so many doctors and nurses in his room they thought a staff meeting was being held. They were merely listening to Casey.

"The doctors examined me from top to bottom," he said. "They didn't miss a thing. They found some of my organs were maybe havin' a slump an' some that were okay. An' they found some which they said I should leave to a medical museum when I pass on."

It was a lot rougher with the Mets but it didn't slow him down a bit. Through bad ball games, long losing streaks, hot and humid days and nights, cold days in damp dugouts and long plane rides jammed into the schedule in such a way that it was impossible to get a regular night's sleep, he remained indestructible.

Sometimes it must have been difficult not to doze on the bench during some of those horrendous games, but Casey seldom sat down, seldom stopped pacing the dugout.

At eight o'clock in the morning following the birthday party they opened the hotel dining room for breakfast. The first guest to show up was Casey Stengel.

"Ah, good morning," he said as the waitress approached for his order. "They tell me your ball club here is having a little trouble winning games. What seems to be the matter?"

MARVELOUS MARV'

When he later went out to Sportsman's Park Casey discovered that there wasn't anything the matter with the Cardinals that Marv' Throneberry couldn't cure.

The score was tied 5–5 in the eighth inning of the first game of the Sunday double-header. The Cards had Stan Musial on third base and Ken Boyer on first with two out. As McKenzie, the Mets' pitcher, threw to the plate, Boyer broke for second. Catcher Choo Choo Coleman's peg to second was perfect, and Boyer found himself hung up between first and second. When he turned to go back to first, Rod Kanehl, the second baseman, threw to Throneberry, the first baseman.

Boyer, trapped, started again for second. Throneberry, the ball clenched firmly in his fist, took off after him, never even glancing at Musial, who had edged carefully off third. Now, seeing Throneberry had no one on his mind but Boyer, Stan raced for home and crossed the plate standing up with the winning run. When Throneberry finally gave up the pursuit and tossed the ball to Shortstop Charley Neal for the tag, Musial was at the water fountain getting a swallow.

Minutes later the Mets' dugout was deserted by all save Stengel. He sat there numb, staring out at the field while Lindsay Nelson asked him to come over and cut himself a hunk of the huge birthday cake the St. Louis management had sent over.

"I keep tellin' myself I'm dreamin' these terrible things that happen," he said. "But I ain't."

In truth, Marv' Throneberry, obtained from the Baltimore Orioles, for whom he did little but pinch-hit, was almost the only player booed by the highly sympathetic Polo Grounds fans. Then one day Frank Thomas, playing third base and having his troubles, twice threw the ball away. The fans gave him a rousing booing as he slumped into the shadows of the dugout.

"Hey, what are you tryin' to do," asked Marv', "steal my fans?"

Throneberry was sometimes jeered after a home run while other members of the club were glorified if they drew a base on balls.

"Ya' got no business bein' up here, Throneberry," they'd yell. "Gowan back to the Yankees!"

"Hey, Marvelous Marv', if you weren't so old you'd be a great Little League player!"

Name any game after he replaced a crippled Gil Hodges in mid-May, and Marv' probably bungled a play in it with disastrous results or did something in the field or on the base paths that, while it didn't affect the outcome, made strong men blanch. He had the knack.

One of his weaknesses was a baseball in his hands when the play was somewhere other than first base, with which he was fairly familiar. If he had to throw to the plate to rub out a runner he might study the situation so long the ball would arrive after the man crossed it. This happened in Houston, in a game the Mets were winning, 3–2 in the ninth—until the Colts scored two runs, the second one as

Larker came in from third when Marv' took what was practically a time-out to throw. The result was Craig Anderson's sixteenth straight loss.

It happened again in Cincinnati. The Reds had Frank Robinson on third and Don Pavletich on second with one out, when Hank Foiles hit sharply to Throneberry. Marv' had his choice, he could go for an easy inning-ending double-play by way of second or he could cut Robinson down at home. He thought it over carefully then threw home just after the runner had slid safely across the plate.

Then there was the game in St. Louis that Al Jackson was winning 1–0 in the ninth inning. Ken Boyer got a hit past third when Feli Mantilla went the wrong way for the ball, something he was very good at. Joe Christopher, who had replaced Frank Thomas in left field for defensive purposes, couldn't find the handle on the ball and Boyer reached second. Jackson was too much pitcher for the next two hitters, however, and suddenly he was only one out away from a rare victory. Now he got Red Schoendienst to lift a high foul near first base. Throneberry yelled that he had it so that nobody else would horn in on his big moment. He moved under the ball carefully and held up his glove. The ball hit the side of it and rolled away. Jackson sighed and walked Schoendienst.

The next Cardinal batter, Bob Zhitfield, lined briskly back to the box. Jackson grabbed it somehow and then, resisting the temptation to run over to first base with the ball, gave Throneberry another chance. He threw the ball. Marv held on to it.

"I knew you could do it, Marvelous!" yelled Jackson as they started for the clubhouse.

Marv' nodded happily.

One of Throneberry's real big days had to be June 17, when the Mets contributed both games of a double-header with the Chicago Cubs to one of their lesser losing streaks.

It started with one of Marv's merry misadventures on the base paths in the first game. Again he had a runner caught in a rundown between first and second. This time he didn't have a man on third base to worry about, if he was in the mood for worrying, so he could concentrate on the man in front of him, Don Landrum.

He threw to the second baseman, then when Landrum reversed his field and started back toward first base. Marv' caught the second baseman's return. Landrum again started for second. This was fun. Marv' ran toward Landrum, saw he couldn't catch him in time, and threw to the second baseman again. Once more Landrum raced back toward first. Throneberry threw him a solid block for no gain. Unfortunately, he didn't have the ball for a tag. The umpire called Landrum safe because of interference.

No matter. Marv' went up to hit after the Cubs had scored four fat runs determined to make amends. Two Mets were on base when his bat caught the ball and drove it toward the bullpen in right centerfield, a certain three-base hit sailing between two outfielders. Marv' put his head down, and raced for first. Rounding the base as though it had a stick of dynamite under it, he picked up steam and headed for second. As the right fielder picked up the ball he tore around second and made for third. The crowd roared as he made third and stood on the base smiling happily.

Ernie Banks, the meanie, called for the ball. When he got it the Cub first baseman stepped on the bag. The umpire jerked up his hand in the out motion. Marv' had neglected to touch first base.

Throneberry had no sooner gone to the dugout, shaking his head in disbelief than Charley Neal hit the left field façade for a home run. Before Neal had taken two steps toward first base Casey Stengel raced out of the dugout. He yelled to Neal, pointed to first base and stamped his foot. Then he pointed to second and stamped again. Then he pointed to third and stamped. Finally he pointed to home, and again brought his foot down. When Neal stepped on home plate Casey nodded gravely and returned to the bench. The customers thought it was great.

It was about August that the tide began to turn for big, balding, round-faced Throneberry. Instead of jeers he heard cheers at the Polo Grounds. The boners were ignored. The throws he didn't hold were overlooked. They roared approval when he caught easy pop flies. And his hits brought down the house.

On August 8 the Mets dropped a double-header to the Pittsburgh Pirates at the Polo Grounds, 9–4 and 8–6. The second was their twenty-first defeat in twenty-four games. But the fans weren't too unhappy. They had seen Marvelous Marv' hit a pair of homers, the second one with two out in the ninth.

When umpire Frank Walsh chased Solly Hemus, the third base coach, off the field in the fifth inning of a game with the Pirates on August 21, Stengel shifted Cookie Lavagetto, his first base coach across the diamond and asked Gene Woodling to coach at first. Then he had to use Woodling as a pinch-hitter and he needed a first base coach again.

"Somebody go out there," said Casey in the dugout.

Ashburn sitting in the corner nodded to Throneberry. "Who me?" asked Marv'. Ashburn nodded.

Throneberry trotted out to the coaching lines. At the sight of him the Polo Grounds people roared.

Came the ninth inning and the Mets rallied. They had lost their thirteenth game in a row earlier in the afternoon, 8–6, when the Pirates overtook them with four runs in the ninth. Ashburn began it with a single and subsequently scored. Then Christopher and Hickman hit safely.

"We want Marvelous!" chanted the fans, "We want Marvelous!"

Stengel called Throneberry in to the dugout and patted

him on his rump as Marv' picked his bat out of the rack. He faced Elroy Face, who had saved the first game for the Pirates. There were two out. It was all up to Marvelous. He hit a three-run homer into the right field seats and the Mets had the game, 5–4. It was marvelous indeed.

By this time Throneberry was getting more mail than all the Mets, the manager, the coaches and the front office put together. Banners bearing his name could be seen all over the Polo Grounds. So could fans wearing "Marvelous Marv" T-shirts. A Marvelous Marv' Throneberry Club had 5,400 members.

At season's end they called him to home plate and wheeled out a $6,000 luxury cruiser. It was Marv's very own because he had hit a circle on a Howard Clothes sign on the right field fence more times than any other Met.

The Howard people also presented Ashburn with a boat that afternoon, because he had been voted the most valuable Met of the season by the sportswriters.

They posed happily for pictures beside their boats.

"What you gonna' do with yours?" asked Ritchie.

"Search me," answered Marv'. "I live in Collierville, Tennessee. The nearest water is the Wolf River about eight miles from my house. An' it's too big for our bathtub. How about you?"

"You think you got trouble," said Ashburn. "I live on a prairie in Nebraska!"

A day later Judge Bob Cannon, legal advisor for the major league ball players, had news for Marv':

"When you make out your 1962 income tax," he told him, "you must declare the full value of that boat. You earned it. Ashburn's is different. He was voted his boat."

"I don't think I'll ever forget this season," said Marv' afterward. "I win a boat but it costs me money. I think I'll go home and try and forget the whole year. Make like it never happened."

Casey Stengel was in Washington for the 1962 All Star game, along with Richie Ashburn, the Mets' only other representative. Freddie Hutchinson, manager of the National League team, had asked Stengel to be one of his coaches.

Just three weeks before his seventy-second birthday, he coached the full nine innings at first base, jogging to and from the lines at each half inning. He hadn't been on the coaching lines since he ran the Oakland club in the Pacific Coast League in 1948.

The Nationals lost the game to the American Leaguers, and Casey said after it was over, "Here I was coachin' these wonderful All Stars, an' what happens? *They* don't get enough hits either. It was just like another game with the Mets."

As Casey started for the first base coaching box in the eighth inning, Joe Cronin, president of the American League, beckoned him over to the official box and introduced him to President Kennedy.

"We talked just a little an' he asked about the Mets," said Casey," an' then about this here game, an' I told him I wasn't managin' this All Star team, so I couldn't say much. I told him I was workin' for Mr. Hutchinson an' I had to get back on the coachin' lines."

When the Sporting News asked its correspondents around the major leagues to describe their biggest thrill of the 1962 season, Harold Rosenthal, its man with the Mets, wrote:

"My biggest thrill came far from the playing field in the form of a pre-dawn tribute to Casey Stengel. I'll never forget it, because it was the first time I heard cheering and yelling in a hotel at four o'clock in the morning and didn't mind it a bit."

The Mets had been demolished 18 to 7 by the Dodgers in a night game in Los Angeles. Their chartered plane for

San Francisco was late in leaving and later still in arriving. Instead of reaching the Jack Tar Hotel in San Francisco at two A.M., as planned, they got in at four.

Instead of a deserted lobby, however, they were greeted by several hundred women of assorted shapes, ages and squeals. Members of various California women's clubs, in convention there, had been alerted earlier by the "Welcome New York Mets" Banner hoisted high on a wall. Now they wanted to see just one man—Casey Stengel. He answered their applause with a speech in which he said he was sorry his club wasn't doing better—and went on from there. At times he was surrounded by so many admiring ladies you could only see his arm waving aloft now and then as he talked.

THE TWO BOB MILLERS

Once there were two Robert Millers, both pitchers, both nice guys and both on the Mets.

Robert G. Miller was lefthanded and he had once pocketed a $50,000 bonus to sign with the Detroit Tigers. Later he pitched for the Reds, who traded him along with third baseman-outfielder Cliff Cook to the Mets for Don Zimmer.

Miller, who had appeared in only six games for Cincinnati, went home. He said at age 29, there was no future for him in baseball and certainly none as a Met.

Wid Mathews, the Mets chief mid-western scout, thought there was still some pitching left in Miller. He went to Zanesville and talked to the man. Among other sales pitches, he reminded Miller that he needed only 18 days to qualify as a five-year man under the pension plan. That meant $125 a month after he reached fifty.

"You go to our Syracuse farm, get into shape and show some pitching. We'll call you up and you can qualify for that pension," said Mathews. "That's found money."

Miller went to Syracuse. He didn't set the International

League on fire, but he did pitch well enough for the Mets to think he might help. The way the Met pitchers were doing about that time, a scrubwoman with a sore arm would have helped.

On July 24 in Milwaukee, Robert G. Miller's Big Moment arrived. The Mets found themselves in need of a fresh pitcher with the score tied 4–4 in the twelfth inning.

Whenever the phone would ring in the New York bullpen, Red Kress, the Mets' coach, would answer it. Sometimes Casey Stengel would be brief and say something like:

"I'm afraid we're blowin' another one. Who we got out there?"

"Only Soanso," Kress would answer. "He's the only one ready. The other two got stiff arms."

"Oh, fer crimp's sake!" Stengel would agonize. "Only Soanso? Tell him to go in the clubhouse an' eat his sandwich. If I blow it I'll blow with what I got out there now."

Then one day Red's answer was that Miller, the new one from Syracuse had been warming up.

"Send him in," commanded Casey, "but be sure an' point him in the right direction. He may not know the way."

Miller took his warm-up pitches, nodded that he was ready, and Del Crandall, the big Milwaukee catcher, took his stance at the plate. Miller pitched, Crandall swung and the ball flew over the left-field wall.

Robert Lance Miller, a righthander with a live arm, had also been a bonus baby, getting a fat bonus from the St. Louis Cardinals in 1957.

On September 10 at the Polo Grounds, it looked as though Miller the righthander, who had lost 11 straight as a Met and won not at all, might be able to walk to the clubhouse a winning pitcher if his companions could rustle up some late runs.

But in the seventh, Hank Aaron broke the 2–2 tie with

a home run and Eddie Mathews hit another with two on, and there was poor Miller 0 and 12.

The two Bob Millers got their mail, their phone calls and their playing cues all mixed up. Stengel would call the bullpen for "Miller" to start heating up his arm and the wrong one would invariably get up. The problem was not solved until Robert G. Miller was sent back to Syracuse, but not before he had stayed long enough to qualify for that pension plan.

Stan Musial thought of retiring at the end of the 1961 season. After all, he was 41, and had all the aches and pains a veteran gets when he has to force himself. He also had a fine steak house business in St. Louis and enough money to live like a millionaire, junior grade.

Then they invented the Mets. Stan looked at the pitching staff that had been rounded up for the new club and drooled at the thought of the hits he could get if he stayed on; all thoughts of quitting fled his mind. He went right down in the cellar and began to bone his bats.

Soon the Cardinals' front office announced that Musial was signing his 1962 season, and that he anticipated a good year.

"He also said something about how nice it would be to play 18 games with the Mets," said a Cards' spokesman, "nine of them at the Polo Grounds, which used to be one of his favorite parks."

The Cards opened the season with the Mets in St. Louis. Musial got three hits off Roger Craig. He went on from there to bat .468 against them for the season. In 13 games he got 22 hits, four of them home runs and batted in 15 runs. That helped him fashion a .330 average for the season, the third best batting mark in the National League. Only Tommy Davis, of the Los Angeles Dodgers, who led with .346, and Frank Robinson, of the Cincinnati Reds with .342, did better.

Warren Spahn, the old smoothie, was shopping for his 313th major league win in the first game and almost had it in his hip pocket 2–1 with two out in the ninth, when a Met got on base. Hobie Landrith, the catcher, hit a fly down the left field line that just made the stands, 279 feet away—for the ball game, 3–2.

There were 19,000 people in the stands. They sounded like 119,000, and they were to bust the sound barrier again some four hours later when Gil Hodges came to bat with the score tied 7–7 in the ninth and hit a homer that made it because the stands are 22 feet shorter in right field.

Two days later a bases-loaded walk to Landrith beat the Cubs in the thirteenth. Mets won five more, including three straight in Milwaukee, before their big decline set in. Starting May 21 at Houston, they went on a seventeen-game losing streak. Two days later they were back in the cellar again. They never again escaped.

The Mets were in the middle of this sad-sack stretch when the Dodgers and the Giants came to town for the first time. The Dodgers beat them three times and the Giants four.

A monster crowd of 55,000, the largest at the Polo Grounds in 20 years, saw the Dodgers win the Memorial Day double-header, 13–6 and 6–5.

Still the cheers went to the Mets. Hodges hit three homers, two in the second game, to move into a tie with Ralph Kiner for tenth place among the all-time home run hitters. And in the sixth inning of the second game, Elio Chacon triggered a historical development.

He made a leaping one-handed catch of Willie Davis's liner; flipped to Charley Neal to get Maury Wills at second; and Neal's throw, in turn, was quick enough to Hodges to make the big put-out before Junior Gilliam could get back to first. An alert Cooperstown recorded the Mets' first triple play.

The Mets were on a baby losing streak, a five-gamer, when they suddenly began to show unexpected muscle. Beginning with a 7–5 decision in Philadelphia on May 6, they won nine out of 12 games, four of them before delirious Polo Grounds fans. They finished their drive by taking two out of three games from Milwaukee, the last two a Sunday double-header. They came close to taking all three, for after the Braves had scored four runs in the ninth, the Mets came back with three of their own and had the bases loaded when Nottebart slipped a disastrous third strike over on Charley Neal.

LITTLE HOT DOG

Elio Rodriquez Chacon played 110 games at shortstop that first season. He stole 12 bases, more than anyone else in the club. He also asked for the most passes to be left at the gate. He wore the gaudiest clothes, consumed at least a dozen bottles of soda pop a day and got into a fight with Willie Mays of the Giants that was nationally televized.

A small, sturdy man with soft eyes and quick movements, Chacon carried a Spanish-English dictionary around with him but the suspicion was that he never opened it. Nape Reyes, the old New York Giant infielder, was asked about him. Reyes had been his manager when Cincinnati operated Havana and Jersey City farm clubs in the International League.

"He always buy clothes," said Reyes. "In one season buy twelve pair crazy shoes, fourteen sports jacket, how many hats? We call heem 'Little Hot Dog.' Chacon nice boy but crazy—clothes-crazy."

When the club got to New York Chacon promptly acquired a bright-colored sports car. A week after the opening of the season, Tom Meany spotted it outside the Polo Grounds. Both headlights and one taillight were smashed, two fenders were twisted, one door handle was missing and there was a crack in the windshield.

"How'd all that happen?" he asked.

"Parking," replied Elio.

That first spring Stengel had been trying to decide where Elio Chacon, the infielder-outfielder with the built-in motor, would best fit.

"Where," asked Casey aloud one morning, "should I play him?"

"Venezuela," answered a hardened sceptic.

It was the seventh inning of the first game of a double-header the Mets lost in San Francisco on May 27. Willie Mays was on first base when a pitch by Roger Craig hit Orlando Cepeda, making him very mad. He began yelling at Craig after reaching first base. Roger, who owns one of the best pick-off moves in the business, wheeled suddenly and threw to Ed Bouchee, his first baseman. Cepeda, caught well off the base, scrambled back. He made it safely only because Bouchee dropped the ball.

Craig here reminded himself that Bouchee was probably even a bigger risk than Throneberry, and that it might be wiser to try and pick Mays, the lead-runner, off second. He threw to Chacon, who ran over from his short-stop position. Mays, sliding back, nicked Chacon with his spikes. One second later Chacon was up and belting Mays. A man of peace, Mays simply picked the smaller man up and threw him to the ground.

Meanwhile the field had become the scene of a free-for-all. When Chacon and Mays began, Cepeda rushed over and started throwing punches at Craig. About them milled other players, coaches and umpires, some of them even trying to stop the show.

A peace of sorts was finally restored. Chacon, the umpires decided, had been the instigator. He was told to take his bad manners to the clubhouse. Play was resumed with Cepeda, at first base, yelling promises of more action to Craig. Roger, knowing he still had his man angry enough to be careless, decided to give Bouchee another chance. Again his quick throw caught Cepeda leaning the wrong way. But again Bouchee dropped the ball.

The Mets collapsed under four Giants runs, in the eighth, 7–1. Then they lost the second game, 6–5.

Immediately afterward they boarded a plane for New York, where they were to play seven straight games with the Dodgers and Giants, starting with a Memorial Day double-header. Chacon sat silent in his seat obviously upset. He knew that Willie Mays was tremendously popular in New York, that the game featuring his fight with Willie had been televised there, and he wondered what his reception would be.

"Weel they boo?" he asked plaintively.

Al Jackson earned a special place in Mets history on April 29 when he became their first shutout pitcher. He beat the Phillies 8–0 before 20,000 Polo Grounds witnesses. He was to pitch three more shutouts.

Jackson's a little fellow, but he's the Bobby Shantz type, the complete ball player. In addition to pitching, he can hit, bunt, field his position well and run the bases swiftly and alertly. As a schoolboy at Moore High School in Waco, Texas, he was an outfielder and a T-formation quarterback.

He was a good enough footballer to attract a number of scholarship offers. He settled for Wiley College, in Marshall, Texas.

As one of a number of teammates who had to be grateful the Mets came into being, he had spent four years in the obscurity of the Pittsburgh farm system.

"Every time they'd say to me that I had the makings of a good pitcher but needed more seasoning."

Casey Stengel liked him from the start. "He executes a lot of things right," said the manager that first spring. "I heard he was a curveball pitcher when we drafted him but the young man tells me he throws a sinker. Why, that's what made Whitey Ford a great pitcher last year. You have a lefthanded pitcher with a sinker, you got a pretty good pitcher."

He won eight games in 1962, an extraordinary performance considering that four of them were shutouts and considering the unskilled labor he had behind him most of the time. The wins were sometimes spaced far apart.

"I haven't won a game in more than a month," he moaned after a particularly tough defeat. "I sit up nights thinking about a game before I pitch. I know I'm pressing too much but I want to win so bad . . ."

Once he had a 3–1 lead going into the ninth. Then he hit Felipe Alou and Willie McCovey in succession. Willie Mays flied out and Alou moved to third. Jackson got Orlando Cepeda to hit what should have been a double-play ball to shortstop. Larry Burright let it bounce off his glove and Alou scored. Then Jim Davenport hit a two-run double for the ball game, 4–3.

Jackson's pitching was much better on June 22 at the Polo Grounds and so was his defense. Working the first game of a twi-nighter with Houston, he held the Colts to one hit in winning 2–0.

It was a dream game and might have easily been a no-hitter. The second man in the Houston batting order, Joey Amalfitano found him for a single in the first inning. Norman Larker, the fourth batter, walked. Nobody else got on base until Pidge Brown, pinch-hitting, drew a pass to open the ninth. Jackson struck out nine.

"If I hadn't been playing in for a bunt by Amalfitano I might have had a chance at his shot," said Felix Mantilla, the third baseman.

They pulled one hair-raiser behind Al. In the eighth Chacon went well back of second base to literally overtake a sizzler off Hal Smith's bat, give it the backward flip to Charley Neal as he went by, and then turn to see Neal relay to first base to catch the hitter.

Jekyll and Hyde ball players, the Mets had no sooner finished their fancy 2–0 win, than they went into reverse and absorbed a 16–3, 17-hit shellacking from the Colts in the second game.

The way other managers sometimes acted when their teams were beaten by Casey Stengel's, it was as if they didn't think the Mets were members of the human race. Gene Mauch steamed when it was suggested in Florida that his Phils, who had lost a record 23 games in a row and finished in the cellar for the fourth season in succession the year before, might be a team the Mets could beat. He showed greater aggravation when the Mets won two games of their first series at the Polo Grounds, one on Al Jackson's 8–0 shutout.

Mauch is a mild man in defeat, however, compared to Fred Hutchinson of the Cincinnati Reds. A hard loser as a pitcher, he had an even lower boiling point as a manager.

The Reds, who had won the National League pennant the year before, had gotten off to a disappointing start. At one point, early in the season, they were 12 games out of first place. Then in mid-May, they began to move, and were only a game-and-a-half behind when they came to the Polo Grounds for a four-game series.

They won the first game 8–6 and Hutch was a fairly happy man. Then the Mets took a double-header, 9–1 and 3–2. They followed this up by winning the first game of another double-header the next day, 5–2, Al Jackson working a five-hitter.

Like the Mets, the Reds trudged the length of the field for the clubhouse and a between-games snack. Hutchinson, though, stayed in the dugout, staring stonily at the floor.

"I was so mad," he said afterwards, "I couldn't trust myself in the clubhouse."

The Reds returned in early August and this time the Mets won the series from them, two out of three. The last game went to the Mets, 8 to 2, and once again Hutchinson sat in the dugout for a long time afterward, cooling off in the dusk.

"I saw Casey Stengel in Toots Shor's that night," said Hutch, "and he offered to buy me a drink. I said no thanks real polite like because I wasn't quite as mad by then. But imagine, in Cincinnati we won nine straight from them, and in the Polo Grounds we lost three out of five in August and two out of three in September.

"In those three September games they scored 24 runs against us. Imagine that. And Bob Purkey and Jim O'Toole were two of our best pitchers. They got ten runs off us in the first game, six in the second and eight in the third."

The Reds were only three games behind the Giants and Dodgers when the season ended.

Out on Long Island, not far from where they were building, in stop-and-go fashion, the new home for the Mets, the citizens could hardly wait for the first season to end and a bright new one to begin.

More than 400 people crowded the grand ballroom of a hotel in Garden City, Long Island, for a *Nassau County Welcomes the Mets* wing-ding. Leonard Hall, national chairman of the Republican party, was toastmaster and Casey Stengel, of course, the principle speaker.

"I want to say this is a treee-mendous thing," Casey began, "with all you people who musta' been followers of the Brooklyn Dodgers showin' up to adopt the Mets. It also shows that you have treeee-mendous spirit in not swearin' off us for losin' so many games an' that you know we are doin' our best—with no help from those big-hearted owners of the other National League clubs who give us only their ball players which need Blue Cross—to build a ball club you can be proud of."

Among the notables on the dais at this affair was Marv' Throneberry, first baseman, outfielder and now, because of his frequently extraordinary accomplishments, a man-about-banquets.

Sometime between the soup de jour and the demitasse, Jonathan Daniel, a young fan sitting at a nearby table, waved a baseball for his attention.

"Sign this Marv', please?" he shouted.

Throneberry nodded and held up his hands. The boy tossed the ball to him.

Marv' dropped it.

MAN IN THE MIDDLE

The long, long season ended in Chicago on September with a 5–1 loss at the hands of the Cubs. It was the Mets' 120th defeat.

"I have to say it wasn't any fun," Casey Stengel announced after the game, "It had to be bad. I had to get used to losing all over again. It was worse than in those seasons in Brooklyn an' Boston. It was shocking because we didn't win at least 50 games. There were at least [10 easy lost that should have been won. Imagine 40 games I won with this club—40. That's what I used to lose with the Yankees!"

Richie Ashburn played second base that afternoon and, with Marv' Throneberry, fashioned a double-play. Then he went home to Tilden, Nebraska, called up an advertising agency and told them he'd be happy to take the broadcasting job in Philadelphia they'd talked to him about several times during the season.

In the Polo Grounds the man in the middle always had to be one who could range far on the defense. It wasn't so important that the centerfielder be able to hit the long ball as to catch it. That's why the Mets took Ashburn from the Cubs. He had roamed centerfield so well that he set a number of major league records for defensive work, like nine seasons in which he had 400 or more putouts, including four in which he made more than 500 putouts, another record.

The white-haired Nebraskan, one of the original Philadelphia Whiz Kids, no longer owned blazing speed. The legs were no longer fleet, the reflexes no longer fresh.

"We know Ashburn is not as fast as he once was," said Johnny Murphy, correlator of all Mets scouting reports. "He'll soon be 35 years old. But he is still faster than most players in the National League. When Solly Hemus managed the Cardinals last season he saw a lot of him, and Solly tells us that Richie can still play an awful lot of centerfield."

He was what the trade calls a "pesty" hitter. Only the pitchers of the National League really appreciated what a pest he was. Joe DiMaggio, Hank Greenberg, Bill Dickey, Bill Terry, Mickey Cochrane, Joe Cronin and Gabby Hartnett, some pretty prominent baseball names, have two things in common. All of them are in baseball's Hall of Fame and none of them made as many hits as Ashburn.

Ashburn owned 2,455 hits when he opened the season with the Mets. He added 119 in the 135 games he played for them. He batted .306, the only Met able to reach the .300 mark.

A wit, raconteur and prominent young Nebraska Republican, Ashburn was a joy to the journalists who traveled with the Mets. They would board a plane wearily after hammering out the sad story of another loss on their typewriters and there, ready to talk on all cylinders, would not only be Casey Stengel, but Ashburn.

"I've been on some winning ball clubs and I've been

on some losers," Richie was saying during one flight, "but none of them ever tries any harder than this one.

"I'm trying to make a hit every time I go to bat," he continued thoughtfully, puffing on his pipe, "and I'm trying to make every play I'm in good. I think most of the players feel the same way.

"A lot of people probably think nobody on this club could play on a contending club. Well, I think there are some guys on contending clubs who couldn't play for us. A lot of people probably think of us as rejects and the guys resent it. Most of us feel we could play for good clubs, maybe the Yankees.

"You know it takes courage to go out there and get beaten. Anybody can go out there and win. There's a lot of pressure on us, more than on a club up in the pennant race. It's a lot easier playing for a winner than playing on a losing club.

"Do I miss the feeling of being with a club up in the race? I can't say I like losing. But you just can't let that feeling get you. If you did you should quit. Our guys have pride. Nobody wants to do bad. There are days, you know, when this is a damn good ball club. Trouble is there just aren't enough of those days.

"Play for the Mets? I wouldn't have missed it for anything. I'll never forget the way those Polo Grounds fans act no matter how badly we're doing. They could make it real miserable for us, but they don't."

One day early in the season Ashburn, walking the outfield grass from the centerfield clubhouse in the Polo Grounds to the Mets' dugout, was hailed by a fan in one of the field boxes behind first base.

The man introduced himself. He said his wife, who had never seen a major league ball game before the arrival of the Mets, was now an enthusiastic fan and that he, of all Stengel's troops, was her favorite.

"She even heard they used to call you 'Mr. Putt Putt' down in Philadelphia," he said, "and now she yells it all the time. Maybe you've heard her.

"She isn't here today," he went on, "because she had an appointment with the doctor. You see she's expecting a baby. But she gave me a message for you. She wants to name our first child after you. We'll both be here in the same box tomorrow night and she'll stand up and wave when you come across the field, so will you please wave back to her?"

Ashburn said it would be a pleasure, and the next night he and expectant mother exchanged smiles and waves. Coming closer Richie yelled to her, "I hope it's quadruplets!"

UP THE RIVER

On April 22, 1963, the New York Yankees went up along the Hudson River to West Point for their annual exhibition game with the U. S. Military Academy team, a practice begun by John McGraw's Giants many years before and taken up by them when the Giants moved to San Francisco.

Army sent two large buses to the Stadium in the morning. One wasn't needed at all and when the second left it carried, besides the trunks full of uniforms and the bat and ball bags, only Dale Long, the utility first baseman, Harry Bright, the infielder who had just arrived that morning after being bought from Washington, coach Johnny Sain, clubhousemen Pete Sheehy and Pete Previte, a public relations man and two newspaper reporters. All the other Yankees were driving up in their own cars.

They lunched with the Cadets, Mickey Mantle first reading the Orders of the Day. Then they went out to the ball field and beat the Academy, 15 to 2.

On May 7, the Mets made their first visit to West Point. Army again sent two buses. Both were filled to capacity; the first with the bachelor ball players or those whose families weren't East with them. The second was jammed with Mets and their wives and children. Two strollers for tiny ones were folded and put in the baggage rack. When the bus unloaded near the Parade Grounds it looked as though a group of farm-belt Congressmen and their families had come to picnic.

It was pleasant but no picnic. The cadets liked the Mets so well they didn't want them to leave.

Before they entered the mess hall for lunch, the Mets grouped out in front watching the companies march in to the music of a band. Casey Stengel stood apart from the rest, rocking on his heels, his hands clasped behind his back. Suddenly the bandsmen began to play something that sounded vaguely familiar. The Cadets as they marched, grinning broadly, broke into song:

"My beer is Rheingold the dry beer"—the Mets' beer sponsor's commercial.

"They've been following the Mets as closely as any group of fans," said Joe Cahill, then director of sports publicity at the Military Academy. "They even have the results of the previous night's Mets game read to them during Orders of the Day. You should hear the cheers when the Mets win."

At lunch they shouted for Casey Stengel to read the Orders.

"The class in geometry has been moved up from 11:25 to 13:35," he began, "which means the class in mechanics of fluids shoulda' been first but in case there's any mistake on account of the Mets bein' here don't worry about it."

Casey kept right on going and could have talked indefinitely but the cadets get only 35 minutes for lunch, and they'd already held the roast beef so long the mess officer was afraid it might be on the condemned list before Casey finished.

The brass admitted afterward that the manager of the Mets was an entertaining speaker, but a colonel was overheard to say that if Casey had read the Orders of the Day at Bunker Hill we'd still be sending our income tax returns to London.

Lunching with the officers, Casey reminded them that as Seaman First Class Charles Dillon Stengel he was just another sailor aboard the U.S.S. Manhattan, a troop ship that carried recruits from the Albany depot to the Brooklyn Navy Yard in 1918.

"We passed West Point comin' an' goin' many times," he said. "We followed the same route as the old Albany Night Boat but our passengers didn't have as much fun. They were just recruited into the Navy when we took 'em aboard an' they wished they weren't by the time we landed 'em in Brooklyn."

Stengel's previous visit to West Point was as outfielder with John McGraw's New York Giants in the spring of 1923.

McGraw always split his squad into two teams for the exhibition games traveling north from their Texas training base. One March he had called Casey in for a talk.

"I've heard you say you want to be a coach some day," he told him. "Well I'll teach you all I can. Now for a starter, we have this young Jimmy O'Connell in camp. He cost us $75,000, so I want to see as much of him as I can this spring. I'm going to keep him in centerfield with the regulars. I already know what you can an' cannot do, so I'm sending you with the B squad. Only you're to be in charge of it, run it like a manager."

The B squad played a lot of exhibition games from Florida up. Casey would get the newspapers here and there and read that O'Connell was going great with the first team. He began worrying about his job. "I finally wrote McGraw a letter sayin' I thought it was time I rejoined the first team so I'd be in better shape to play for him or for some other club if I was traded. I said someone else could run the B team better, 'specially Cozy Dolan, the coach, an' that I was lettin' Cozy run the team the rest of the way."

When Casey rejoined him at West Point, McGraw was mad about that letter.

"Did you sign a manager's contract to manage my B team?" he asked.

Casey admitted that he had not.

"Well then how could you resign from the job if you had no contract?" he asked. "Now I'll tell you what I'm gonna do. When we leave West Point after the game I'm gonna' leave you here to tell these officers an' Cadets all about the Giants. I don't want to see you until we open the season."

Getting back to the Mets' West Point day, the Cadets proved stiff opposition for them once the game began. When the sixth inning arrived without either team having scored, George Weiss sitting behind the home plate screen called an assistant.

"I know it was agreed that we'd play a seven-inning game," he said. "But the fans might not like it if the game was called with the game scoreless like this. I think it would be wiser if we announced that the game would go on until one side or the other scored, then be called. Better call Lavagetto or one of the other coaches over and have them get together with Eric Tipton, the Army coach."

But the sixth inning went by without a run and the Cadets in the stands began to dream of an Army victory over a team with a major league label. In the seventh, however, the Mets managed to fashion three runs, Weiss relaxed and the game was called.

Col. Red Reeder, author, soldier, trencherman and assistant athletic director at the Academy, recalled Stengel's 1923 visit. He was the Army first baseman then.

"Casey got a hit," recalled Red. "And after he reached first base he nudged me.

" 'Got a chaw of tobacco to spare, soldier?' he asked.

" 'Gosh, no sir,' " I said, " 'That wouldn't be allowed here.'

" 'Then it must be a helluva place!' he said, and *zip* stole second base just like that. I've respected him as a talker ever since."

THE SECOND HORRENDOUS SEASON

The early hopes and hurrahs were forgotten when the Mets started their second season by losing the first eight games. The fans were almost sullen. Some suggested that they were clowns unfit for human association. The day after they lost their eighth, in Cincinnati, a Den Mother in Demarest, N. J. named Pat Barber, called to challenge them to a softball game on behalf of Cub Scout Troop No. 186.

Fortunately they upended Milwaukee, 5–4, on their return to the Polo Grounds, April 19. Not only that but they won the next three from the Braves, and went on to make it eight out of 12. All was forgiven. The banners were held on high again.

One of the wins was a 2–0 shutout of the Cubs in Chicago by Carlton Willey on April 24. He became the first Met righthander in history to fashion a shutout. Statistics like this were broadcast as they are for a man being launched into space.

Willey held the Cubs to three hits and made outs of the last 20 batters to face him. While he was controlling the situation the Mets found Bob Buhl for two runs, the first on successive singles by Thomas, Kranepool and Coleman in the second inning and the second on Hunt's first major league home run in the fifth.

A tall, lantern-jawed, serious citizen of 32, Willey was delighted by the news of his purchase by the Mets during the spring training period. With Milwaukee he seemed to have nothing to look forward to except the same old seat on the bullpen bench. But for the fact that he needed only eight more playing days to qualify for a five-year pension, he might have been tempted to stay in Cherryfield, Maine (population 752), and work in his father's hardware store.

Willey had a fine nine-seven record in half a season with Milwaukee in 1958, four of the victories being shutouts. His earned-run average was a gaudy 2.70. He was named National League Rookie of the Year and he probably couldn't have been bought for $300,000.

But he couldn't escape from the Spahn-Burdette shadow. He rusted from inactivity and, because he wasn't started regularly, slumped to 5–9, 6–7 and 6–12 for the next three seasons.

Nevertheless, Willey finished his season with the Mets with a 9–14 record and would have made it a better one but for three weeks in sick bay with an angry arm. Four of his wins were shutouts.

One of the most notable was a 5–0 job on the Cubs on August 24, the Mets' 41st victory. Among the others who this day helped make it certain the club would be the winningest Met team yet, was Jim Hickman, who started the pitcher off with his 13th home run of the season in the first inning, matching his homer production for 1962. Before the game ended poor Jim also fanned for the 96th time, equaling his previous season's whiff total, which was a team high.

In another game the pitcher, who had been asked to pitch only 73 innings by the Braves the season before, held Cincinnati to five hits and won when Jim Hickman's homer in the eighth fractured a 2–2 tie. This, on the amazing afternoon the Mets made it five in a row, their longest winning streak.

Willey was the homespun hero who, after the Giants had demolished Mrs. Payson's pets 17–4 one sad Saturday afternoon, made believers of 53,000 Polo Grounds spectators by beating the champions 4–2 on Sunday.

He was also the pitcher who threw a three-hit shutout at the Giants in San Francisco, probably his best game of the year. A couple of runners got as far as second base in the first inning and that was it. Tom Haller tried to swipe the base in the second and was rubbed out by Choo Choo Coleman's fine throw. After that there was only one play at second, Jack Sanford being forced by Joey Amalfitano in the fifth.

"I signed with the Braves in 1951 when they were still in Boston," Willey relates. "That was a good deal, since it was near home. Then two years later the franchise was moved to Milwaukee."

It was a break when the Mets bought him and he could move his family back East, but one day in May he must have thought he was still what the ball players call snake-bitten.

His wife Nancy, a social science teacher in Cherryfield, came to New York for a big week-end reunion, bringing their six-year-old son Richie.

"They were no sooner unpacked, than the youngster got sick. My wife called the hotel doctor and it didn't take him long to give her the bad news. Richie had chicken pox. They never got out of the hotel room."

The mailman who had the Polo Grounds on his route must have been a Met fan because he never grumbled at the extra heavy loads he had to carry up the old clubhouse

steps. Packages he delivered after some particularly horrible game must have sometimes made him suspect explosive contents.

Casey Stengel's desk was always piled high with letters
of advice, criticism and praise. The players' fan mail was
also abundant, depending on each man's degree of success
or failure. At the height of his popularity Marv' Throneberry got hundreds of letters a day.

The Mets' mail came from all over and it often included packages that contained good luck charms and
ointments, home-made candies, cookies, preserves, birthday cakes, horseshoes, rabbits' feet and, in one instance, a
large bottle of a secretly concocted snake oil liniment for a
pitcher with a sore arm. A lady in Wilmington, Del., sent
Stengel a large can of dark brown, evil-smelling powder
which, she assured him, would put the batters in Roger
Craig's power if sprinkled over home plate before a game
—this when Roger was struggling with his long losing
streak. A man named Dave Leslie wrote from Point
Pleasant, N. J., offering to come up any weekend and
hypnotize the players. One letter began,

> Dear Sir, you numbskull:
> When are you going to bring back Marv'
> Throneberry like you promised? You are no
> manager in our book if you don't because he
> can't hit in Buffalo and it is stupid for you to
> wait for him to do so because he's affected by the
> cold winds up there and that big ball park. Be
> smart and bring him back to the Polo Grounds,
> where he was just learning how to hit. Be smart
> —for once!
>
>   Yours in sport,
>   Jimmy Davis
> MARVELOUS MARV' THRONEBERRY FAN CLUB,
>   West New York, N. J.

Casey grinned and turned to another. It was written on Monmouth Park Race Track stationery.

"Maybe from one of Mrs. Payson's horses," he said. "We got all kindsa fans." It read:

Dear Casey:

We would like to name a horse after Rod Kanehl, the Met who runs the bases so well. It is a chestnut colt by Safaris-Invariable-Thumbs Up, and is now on our New Jersey farm. As you know, the Jockey Club insists that we must first have the written consent of the person involved. We have already written Kanehl, but Barker Seeley, of Monmouth Park, suggests that we write you too. He says otherwise you might pick up your morning paper and see Rod Kanehl listed among the day's entries at Aqueduct or Monmouth and think Rod Kanehl had jumped the ball club.

Sincerely yours,
Mike Sakele and Joe Sakele.

One day there was a letter from a Huntington, Long Island, matron who was holding a Sweet Sixteen birthday party for her daughter, and she wondered if Mr. Stengel would be so kind as to assign Ed Kranepool, his 18-year-old first baseman, to be her escort for the affair. The young lady's picture was enclosed.

Casey gently laid the letter in the wire basket for someone else to answer and opened another. It was written on the back of a menu from the Post & Coach Inn on Manhattan and bore the signatures of a dozen customers:

Dear Casey:

We hope you are not going to bench Frank Thomas just because some balls have been falling in front of him in left field. We think he is the greatest. We think he belongs in Cooperstown. How does Frank Thomas get in Cooperstown? He takes a bus to Utica, changes for a bus to Cooperstown, walks down the main street until he gets to the Hall of Fame, walks up the stairs and buys a 50-cent admission ticket at the door. He's in, like Flynn.

Yours respectfully,

ARTIE APUZZO.

"There's a match made in Heaven!" exclaimed Tommy Holmes on hearing that the Mets had obtained Jimmy Piersall, the highly combustible outfielder-clown, from the Washington Senators.

Casey Stengel grunted. He needed another comedian like a hole in the head. His big need was hitting and Piersall had hit only .245 for Washington. George Selkirk, the serious citizen who had taken over as Washington's general manager, was happy to unload Piersall—and happier to get Gil Hodges from the Mets at approximately the same time.

Stengel needed someone, however, to catch something in centerfield, and he remembered some stunning defensive plays by Piersall from his days as Yankee manager. It quickly became apparent that Piersall's defensive skills had regressed almost as far as his hitting even though he won the acclaim of the fans with a triple his first day on the job, and by shuffling around the bases backwards when he hit the 100th homer of his career off the Polo Grounds façade.

"Pretty funny," admitted Casey, "but it's even money every laugh that Piersall pulls off now will be topped by my other players sometime during this double-header."

The management was tolerant for eight weeks, then decided the act would no longer be part of the show. Piersall, a .322 hitter with Cleveland in 1961, had batted .194 in 40 games when the Mets asked for waivers on him, got no replies, and gave him his unconditional release.

The year 1963 had started promisingly enough for Marv' Throneberry. He had been voted the annual Ben Epstein "Good Guy Award" as the New York player who had been the most pleasant and cooperative, and in January he was invited to come and accept the plaque at the dinner of the New York chapter of the Baseball Writer's Association at the Hotel Americana.

After various notables had spoken from the dais they began to hand out the awards. When his name was called Marv' made his way through the tables, took the plaque and cracked:

"I was a little afraid to come up and get this for fear I might drop it."

In March, though, he found himself dissatisfied with the contract the club had mailed him and went to Florida at his own expense to see if he couldn't talk it higher.

Throneberry didn't get much work at first base in spring training even after he signed. The club had other plans. Gil Hodges had undergone knee surgery and was only playing now and then. Tim Harkness had come from the Dodgers in a deal.

He got into only 14 games after the season started, mostly as a pinch-hitter, and batted .143.

On a day in May Casey Stengel dreamed up a line-up with five left-handed hitters in it to combat Dick Farrell, the fast Houston righthander. He benched Frank Thomas, his right-handed power hitter (batting average

.190), and put young Ed Kranepool in left field instead.
Then he told Throneberry to play in right.

It was drizzling that night at the Polo Grounds before
the start of the game.

"Good thing, in a way, if I'm to play the outfield,"
muttered Marvelous, "it'll keep the crowd away. There
won't be so many out there to boo me."

The man in charge of sound effects put the Star-Span-
gled Banner platter on at the wrong speed.

"Now I know it's going to be one of those nights," said
Marv' to himself, standing in right field. He was nervous.
He had only played a dozen or so games in the outfield in
his career. He kept praying that if a ball was hit to him it
would be in the air, an easy fly.

Johnny Temple, leading off for Houston, lined the ball
to right field. It was a good hit. Marv' tried to stop when
the ball changed direction on the wet turf, but his legs
went from under him. The ball didn't get through him,
though. It stopped just short of him and he got up and
threw it to second.

Duke Snider had run over from centerfield to lend a
helping hand but all he could do was stand and laugh.

"I thought he'd yell, 'Safe!' when I slid like that,"
said Marv' afterwards. "That's what Ashburn would have
yelled. But he just kept laughing and saying, 'Throw to
second, throw to second.' "

Snider, whom Marv' had been breaking in as his straight
man replacing Ashburn, was coming along nicely in the
comedy bit.

"He's a good golfer," Duke said, "so I couldn't understand why he didn't replace his divots."

"I kept lookin' over to Duke for advice," recalls Marv',
"but every time he saw me look he looked the other way.
I figured it would take a couple of weeks to settle down in
right field."

Throneberry wasn't around that long. Not many days afterward came cutdown time and Marv's name was on the list.

The bat boy edged up to him during batting practice and said Casey wanted to see Marv' and Gil Hodges in his clubhouse office.

"You go in first Gil," Marv' said. "I'll wait on you." He wanted to stay a Met as many minutes more as he could.

Hodges was told that he had been placed on the disabled list. Then it was Marv's turn. He talked to Casey ten minutes and when he came out the news was written all over his face. He walked slowly to his locker, the one with "Marvelous Marv" painted where the other lockers had merely surnames. He sat down and hung his head. Then he reached into his locker for a cigarette and sat silent a long time.

"I was prepared for it, I guess," he said finally. "I could tell when they weren't playing me. Casey said that if I started hitting at Buffalo, they'd bring me back."

He nodded in appreciation each time a teammate or a newspaperman stopped by to tell him they were sorry to hear the news.

Days later, at Yankee Stadium, a man was talking to Ralph Houk, the Yankee manager, about Throneberry. He had been Marv's manager at Denver, a Yankee farm club, for three seasons.

"He was a good first baseman, a good fielder," said Ralph. "Why, I used to use him as my cut-off man on throws from the outfield.

"He had power then comparable to Mantle. I think he hit 195 home runs in six seasons. A streak hitter, though, something like Bill Skowron. He'd carry the whole club with his hitting for a while and then he wouldn't be able to buy a hit for a week.

"When he came up to the Yankees he found he couldn't

break in. He was bucking Skowron, Siebern and others all those years and I guess he got discouraged—also older and he didn't get to play as much. He must have lost his co-ordination, gradually, because of not playing regularly. At Baltimore he had to buck Gentile. And I think he hurt his leg there."

Members of the Marvelous Marv' Throneberry Fan Club and many others didn't cotton to his demotion at all. They wrote letters of indignation to the club and the newspapers. They continued to wear their fan club T-shirts. Officers of the club boasted that it had a special fund set aside to pay for a skywriting plane to spell out, "WELCOME HOME, MARV" over the Polo Grounds on the glorious day he returned. They talked of hiring a helicopter to bring him from Idlewild Airport and set him down somewhere around first base in the Polo Grounds.

June 28 was Throneberry-revisited-day for the Mets. They were in Buffalo for an exhibition game with their farm club. It came as a shock to some of them to learn that Marv' wasn't the Bisons' regular first baseman, that Ed Bouchee sometimes played there instead.

"Some days the Bisons win; other days they play Throneberry," a native had told them rather sourly on arrival.

That night at the ball park the most popular Met ever to make mistakes at the Polo Grounds, put on his best bib and tucker, and his most determined expression and played in the hope that his old ball club would wrap him up and take him along when it left.

Alas, it was one of those games for Marvelous. In the third inning Pumpsie Green, the Buffalo third baseman, fetched Al Moran's grounder and threw on one bounce to first base. The ball ignored Marv's glove and hit him in the chest.

At bat for the first time against Don Rowe, he started hopefully for first base on a three-and-two pitch, but the umpire said the curve had crossed the plate for a third strike. Marv' gave him his most reproachful look, then walked sadly to the dugout.

He got a base on balls the next time up, but fanned on three straight pitches with a man on base in the sixth. In the ninth, with Buffalo rallying, he grounded out weakly.

That's the way it had been going for Marv' at Buffalo. When he went there on May 12, he began getting a couple of dozen fan mail letters of encouragement a day from his New York admirers. Now he was down to two.

CHOO CHOO

Sometimes, after a particularly heart-warming win, the lawn in front of the ancient centerfield clubhouse at the Polo Grounds was reminiscent of the players exit at a college football stadium after a big game. Chanting, cheering customers gathered by the hundreds and wouldn't move until the day's big heroes appeared at the top of the stairs to take a bow.

Jim Hickman had to put his uniform shirt back on and take a curtain call outside after he had become the first Met to hit for the cycle one day against the Cubs. His single, a double, a triple and finally a home run in that order helped humble Chicago 7–3. Two days later he was out there again, except this time he had Roger Craig for company. His grand-slam homer in the ninth had enabled the pitcher to end his long losing streak at 18 games, beating the Cubs 7–3.

Another afternoon it was Choo Choo Coleman, always an object of the fans' affection despite a poor batting average. This day Choo Choo was "on." A big soft liner in short right field scored Al Moran to bust a tie in the twelfth inning, and make Larry Bearnath's first major league decision a winning one over the Cincinnati Reds, 12–11.

It had been a disorderly game. The fans, angered over the loss of the first game of the double-header, began to rain fruit, paper, cardboard containers and other debris on the Cincinnati outfielders. The umpires warned them that the game would be forfeited to the Reds if the downpour didn't stop.

The Mets had scored six time to take an 11–6 lead in the fifth, so their admirers felt better. But when Cincinnati came back with six runs in the sixth they went at it again and had to be warned once more.

A bases-loaded sacrifice fly by Hickman tied it up in the eighth and brought up Coleman. Casey Stengel was on the top step of the dugout, leading the customers in yelling, "Go-Go Choo Choo!" Then, when he saw Coleman almost topple trying to pull the ball, he got his attention and pantomimed a straightaway swing. Choo Choo caught on. His single scored Moran to win it.

Coleman isn't a chatter-box. The words he uses in a day could be written on one side of a half dollar. Explaining the victory afterwards, he said, "We score six. They score six. We score five. They score six. We need two."

To the 500 or so fans outside the clubhouse afterwards he said, "It's nice. First time it ever happened since I play baseball. It's nice."

Coleman had been a Stengel favorite from the start. He sought to build up the young catcher's confidence much as he had Yogi Berra's in his early Yankee years.

"Maybe he wouldn't be on this club if I wasn't the manager," he said, "which might be a mistake. He can make the pitchers look better than the others. He can throw. He can run. He is very alert. He can dig balls out of the dirt an' he backs up first base in a hurry. If he could hit he'd have five points. I think he'll learn."

Ralph Kiner had Choo Choo on his TV show after this big (three singles) day. He knew the shy little catcher didn't talk much, but thought he knew something that would draw him out—his nickname.

He introduced Coleman, talked about his youngsters, mentioned how he was quite a tennis player in Orlando, Florida, during the off-seasons. He recalled Coleman's days as a rookie with the Phillies, chatted about his minor league play with Montreal, Macon, Spokane and Syracuse.

Ralph glanced at the studio clock. Five minutes of the interview were left. Now was the time to spring the question that surely would fill it.

"Choo Choo," he asked, "Tell me, how did you get that nickname?"

Coleman was silent for a minute, then started to speak. Kiner relaxed.

"I don't know," he said.

TIME OUT TALES

It was early afternoon at the Polo Grounds when a good-looking, sandy-haired boy came into the dugout with a man. The Mets were taking batting practice before their game with Pittsburgh and Casey Stengel was down the bench talking to the newspapermen. When he saw the two visitors he hustled down to them in the semi-dogtrot he uses when he wants to take a pitcher out of the box before the fellow faints or something.

"Mike," he shouted, shaking hands with the boy. "How ya' been? It's about time my old friend Mike Blanck came down from Connecticut, which is a nice place an' I can't blame you for not wantin' to leave it much."

"This is my father," said the boy.

"How ya' do?" said Casey. "Mighty fine boy you have here."

"Thank you," said the man. "Mike sure thinks a lot of you, Casey," he said. "Talks and talks about you and the Mets. Knows every batting average on the club, everything about the boys."

"That's good," said Casey. "Maybe he can help me with my managin'. Now Mike, how's school?"

"Fine," replied the boy, "just fine."

"What grade you in now?"

"The eighth," the boy answered, smiling with pleasure over the attention Casey was giving him.

"What's the name of that town you come from," asked Casey, "Fairfield?"

"That's right, you have a good memory, Casey."

"I hafta' have a good one to keep rememberin' the names of all my players, they come an' go so much. I gotta' lot of travelin' men here. They're gonna' make the New York Central rich ridin' from here to Buffalo an' back so much."

"How's the club, Casey?"

"Now, I'm glad you asked me that question, because some days it's not so hot but other days it amazes me, an' I ask you how you gonna' make up your mind with fellas like that? But I have to because I can't be playin' different lineups all the time or the fans'll get more confused than the umpires."

The players were coming in to the bench now, to towel their faces and grab a swallow of water at the fountain. Casey called them over, one by one.

"Mike, you meet all these fellers the last time? I don't think so. Shake hands with Mr. Coleman here. They call him Choo Choo an' nobody includin' himself knows why. Meet Mr. Stallard, who comes from a place in Virginia nobody knows where. An' here's Mr. Kanehl, the hot rod, an' Mr. Snider, who hits those beautiful home runs sometimes. . . ."

"Are you really seventy-three years old, Casey," asked the boy after Stengel had not only introduced him to all the players but the umpires as well.

"Some days yes, an' some days no," answered the manager. "I don't feel that old, though, until my players don't execute right. Where you think I get all these furrows?" Casey took Mike's hand and put it to his face.

Mike laughed and briefly traced the rugged outlines of the Stengel features with his fingers, ran them around his cap and finally found Casey's hand again.

"You're not old," the boy said. "And this club's going to get better, don't you worry. You have some young players who will make real major leaguers with some more experience."

"I'll remember that," said the manager. "An' now ya' better go get a good seat an' see that your father buys you enough peanuts an' popcorn. An' I hope we win one fer ya' so you can tell the fellas at school all about it."

Mike Blanck said he sure hoped the Mets would win too, and left the dugout with his father, who had brought him down from a Connecticut school for blind boys for the day.

The first of the winter baseball meetings were held at Rochester, and before the Met officials went there they called Kerby Farrell, the manager of the Buffalo club, with which they now had a working agreement, to bring along all the dope he had on International League players.

There was a bit of consternation in the Farrell household when the voluminous notes Kerby had taken almost daily in 1962, were not to be found. Desks were searched, drawers emptied, suit-cases searched to no avail. Finally Mrs. Farrell remembered she had told their maid to clean up her husband's den a few weeks ago.

"I remember now she said she was throwing a lot of paper stuff out," she said. "I wasn't paying much attention at the time. Your baseball notes must have been among them."

Luckily Kerby has a 17-year-old son blessed with a retentive memory. He had seen many of the Bisons games and helped his father prepare his notes afterwards. They sat down and between them, went over the names of every player in the league, making notes the while. It took time and much talk and mental mining but gradually they compiled a book on every player. Kerby went to Rochester prepared.

The Mets spent July 1, an off-day on their schedule, helping the good people of Grayslake, Illinois, honor one of its leading citizens, Jay Hook.

The Mets were in last place, had just come off a terrible three-game series in Pittsburgh and had lost nine straight road games, but when they arrived at Grayslake, a pleasant little village in the middle of the Illinois farmland, they were greeted like World Series heroes.

At two o'clock in the afternoon, when the temperature was 110, most of its 2,400 residents lined the sun-blistered main street to cheer the Mets as they rode by in open automobiles. Ahead of them marched four school bands and marching units and some 250 little leaguers.

Bright red banners reading WELCOME JAY, WELCOME METS crossed overhead. Flags waved at close intervals all along the street of single-storied stores. WELCOME METS signs filled the windows, and were painted on the sidewalks and store fronts.

The 26 Hook families in the phone book were present. Jay's dad, Cece, operates Cece's Drug Store. A little further down the street is another drug store run by another Hook. Bob Hook runs a delicatessen, another Hook owns the big lumber yard and yet another a men-and-boys-wear shop.

"At one time," said his father, "people named Pester ran a number of stores on one side of the street and we Hooks had more on the other. Folks used to say they got pestered on one side and hooked on the other."

A sign in the window of Cece's said that in honor of the occasion all milk shakes would be only 19 cents. In addition, all purchasers got an autographed picture of Jay. In

Fischer's a loaf of bread went with every purchase of a dozen eggs.

Hook lingered dowtown signing autographs in the shade of the savings and loan company's WELCOME JAY sign.

A youngster darted out of the group and ran to his mother across the street.

"I got it signed, but it's not him," he said with obvious disappointment. "It's not Casey Stengel."

"Of course not," corrected his mother. "It's Jay Hook. That's who this is all about."

Two days later a large number of Grayslake people journeyed to Chicago to see their boy pitch against the Cubs. It would have been a nice one to win, but this wasn't Jay's day either. He started and others followed, three Mets pitchers being battered for eight runs in the third inning. The Cubs won 9-2.

Mayo Smith, who scouts the clubs in both leagues for the Yankees, dropped in at Wrigley Field the next afternoon, the Fourth of July. He sat behind home plate with a number of scouts from other American and National League Clubs a very interested man; he had never seen the Mets play.

A high throw by third baseman Cliff Cook, which should have resulted in the third out, gave the Cubs a run in the first inning. Then Jim Hickman's home run off Hobie tied it up for the Mets in the sixth.

The two clubs went into the ninth still tied one to one. Craig had allowed just four hits, only one since the fourth, and seemed stronger than ever.

"Say, what's all this junk I've been hearing and reading about the Mets?" asked Mayo. "I mean all that stuff about them being such a bad ball club? Why, these fellows play good ball."

"Wait, just wait," answered Tom Sheehan, scouting for the Giants.

He didn't have long to wait. Ernie Banks began the ninth by grounding to Chico Fernandez. The shortstop booted the ball, then chased it into short left field for a two-base error. Craig, concentrating on keeping Ken Hubbs from bunting if possible, threw low and outside and the curveball bounced away from Norm Sherry, his roommate and favorite catcher. Banks raced for third. Sherry retrieved the ball and threw to third, but on the bounce. Cook couldn't block the ball, and it went out to the Chicago bullpen. Cook was still looking for the ball as Banks crossed the plate with the winning run.

"See what I mean?" said Sheehan.

Williams is the name of a large restaurant on Wabash Avenue in Chicago. It isn't garishly lighted like some because it is a mood place late at night with a pianist pounding out melodies, sometimes singing as she plays.

It had been a tough afternoon for the Mets at Wrigley Field, one of those afternoons a man wants to forget.

Dinner had been late for Casey Stengel. He had gone to his suite to wait for a phone call from George Weiss in New York. They were hopeful of closing the deal for Jesse Gonder, the Cincinnati catcher. Nothing developed that night, however, and Casey left the room and walked to Williams. The place was fairly crowded and everyone turned when Casey entered with his party and stopped just inside the door.

"I'm Casey Stengel," he announced. "I'm manager of the Mets an' we're in trouble!"

People grinned, some of them coming over to shake hands. Conversation at the bar picked up, strangers asking each other how-about-that-Casey-huh? The manager seated the Stengel party at a large booth near where Annette Sachs sat at her piano.

The hours went by and so did the Stengel stories. Kankakee, Montgomery, Brooklyn, Worcester, Selma, New

Orleans, London, Miami, Tokyo, Glendale—five stories at every stop.

Suddenly Casey stopped. The pianist was playing a Gay Nineties melody. This one made him listen. Suddenly tears streamed down his face.

"Is something the matter, Casey?" Jack Lang asked.

"You know," he said, "I first came to Chicago in 1910. I was 18 years old. I'd promised my mother back in Kansas City that I'd write . . . and I never did."

July 30th was Casey Stengel's 73d birthday and the Mets' present to their manager was a handsome 5–1 victory over the Dodgers at Los Angeles that ended their record string of road losses at 22.

They staked Tracey Stallard, the Lil' Abner type, to two runs in the first inning, something that hadn't happened to a Met pitcher since July 3, and he went on to pitch a strong five-hitter.

In the clubhouse Stengel moved to the center of the room as though to make a speech. He didn't. Instead he cut into a huge birthday cake.

"Where'd it come from Casey?" someone asked.

"The Dodgers gave it to me."

"Break up the Mets!" shouted Duke Snider.

"If Casey had a birthday every day we'd win the pennant!" yelled Jesse Gonder.

Everybody laughed. Icing on the cake was the fact that the beaten Dodger pitcher was ex-Met Bob (Righty) Miller.

There had been a big surprise party at Casey's house the day before on a street in Glendale with royal palms. Edna called him from the garden to answer a phantom phone call from George Weiss in New York. He entered a room filled with newsreel and TV cameras, photographers and friends.

He was surprised but hardly speechless. As the mayor of

Glendale hung a be-ribboned key to the city around his neck, he began what was to be the first of about a dozen impromptu speeches. Then he took some of his guests on a tour of the place. He showed them his den lined with plaques, cabinets filled with silver trophies, hundreds of pictures and a painting on one wall depicting a sparrow flying out of a ball player's cap.

"The day I gave them the bird in Brooklyn," he said with a wink.

Out then through Edna's garden and fruit trees to the flower house and swimming pool. Then the tennis court with its pitching machine that serves tennis balls.

"Throws better than some of my pitchers," he remarked. "An' this concrete court is where those agency fellas took those pictures of me an' Miss Rheingold for the beer ads. They didn't have to rent any studio space. Didn't cost them a thing."

One of Casey Stengel's favorite dugout visitors was Aldoria ("Coco") Jarry, of Hull, Quebec. Coco is a sportswriter whose column, titled "Coco Notes," appears in *Le Progress de Hull*. He also writes for *Le Droit* in Ottawa and other Canadian papers. And he writes a lot about Stengel. Casey calls him, "my old ball-headed Frenchman from Canada."

"Mr. Stengel and I get along fine," Coco said on one visit. "My English, eet puzzles him a little but ee's English, eet puzzles me more. We do not understand each other, so we are great friends."

THE GREAT LOSER

Craig Anderson took a 6–4 lead over the Pittsburgh Pirates going into the ninth inning of the first game of a double-header at the Polo Grounds. It looked as though the end of another long losing streak, a dilly of 12 games, was only three outs away.

Anderson, who had lost 13 in a row himself, got the first man out. Then Bob Skinner got an infield hit and Smoky Burgess walked. The manager came out of the dugout, waving to the bullpen for Roger Craig, his top man. The first thing Roger did was walk Roberto Clemento. This filled the bases.

Jim Marshall, who had been with the Mets earlier in the season, was the next batter. He grounded to Felix Mantilla at third base. Now, Mantilla had a certain out at home plate and possibly a double-play if the catcher could relay the ball to first ahead of Marshall.

"Home, home!" hollered Craig.

But Mantilla threw instead to first base, or rather in the general direction of first. The ball went into the right-field corner, three runs scored—and Craig was a 20-game loser.

"I had my mind made up to go home with the ball," said Mantilla afterwards. "Then I got it and threw it away, I don't know why. I wanted to go find a hole in the ground and hide."

Craig lost 24 games, more than any pitcher in the major leagues that first season, and many were lost just like that, though there were others too in which he bombed as hard as anyone on the staff. That's the way it was with Met pitchers. They were either demolished by batters who could hardly wait to get to the plate, or watched helplessly as a well-pitched game went down the drain because their fielders betrayed them with foolish fumbles or thoughtless plays.

Craig, though, suffered more than the others on this shell-shocked staff of losers. The Mets dropped 30 games by one run in 1962 and the tall, thin, ranch-type right-hander was the pitcher of record in six of them. Five of his losses were by scores of 1–0. Nine times the Mets scored not a single run behind him. He got to accept the fact that life with the Mets meant he would have to pitch a shutout to get a tie.

There was the 1–0 game he lost in Milwaukee on a run-scoring single by Ty Cline in the tenth inning. The Mets couldn't even get a man to third base against lefthander Bob Hendley. Only five of them got to first base (four on singles, one on a base-on-balls) and only one got as far as second. They had a team average of .124 at the time.

Craig allowed six singles and three walks through the first nine innings. He started the tenth by giving a base on balls to Lee Maye, a pinch-hitter. Then came one of those Mets plays. Hendley, allowed to bat for himself, attempted a sacrifice bunt. The ball landed on the first-base side of the pitcher's box. Craig was closer to it but first baseman Tim Harkness yelled that he'd take it.

Catcher Norm Sherry shouted to throw to second base

and force Maye there. Harkness was a trifle slow making the play and Maye was called safe. The next batter was Cline and he singled to right, scoring Hendley.

Craig was bitter in the clubhouse, not hearing sympathetic visitors who told how Casey Stengel had praised his pitching—"You can't expect better pitchin' than that."

"Maybe I'm not the best pitcher in baseball," he said, "but I put myself on even terms with anyone I pitch against. Hendley pitched a four-hit shutout, sure. Why can't I? There's no satisfaction in telling yourself you pitched a great game. You must ask yourself, why then didn't I win it?"

But he refused, as always, to complain about others. "That walk to Maye hurt," he said. "I could throw strikes all afternoon but you try to get the corners. You're trying to be careful and not make the pitch too good. But I can't fault that walk really, because it was that pitch I made to Cline that lost it. Cline doesn't like the ball outside. That's where the ball went and it cost me."

In another game he was leading Don Drysdale, the Dodger flame-thrower, 1–0 in the second inning when Tommy Davis led off with a triple and scored because Frank Thomas, playing third base, threw to first instead of home where he had an obvious play.

The Dodgers broke the 1–1 tie in the fourth when Elio Chacon threw away a grounder by Tommy Davis that should have meant the third out of the inning. The next batter, Ron Fairly, then hit the left field foul line pole for a two-run homer.

In the fifth inning, again with two out, Marvelous Marv' Throneberry somehow contrived to field Maury Wills' grounder with his chin, and another Dodger run scored. One of the Dodgers' two earned runs out of their five came when Frank Howard hit the ball into the left field bleachers in the seventh.

"He had a 1–1 tie if they coulda caught the ball," snapped Casey Stengel later. "But that's something they don't do all the time."

Then there was a game at Pittsburgh, in which Richie Ashburn made his 2,500th major league hit, a single, plus another single, which was followed by Frank Thomas' fourteenth homer of the season and his first in 34 games. Things were looking up. Then the Pirates tied it up in the ninth. And in the tenth Bill Virdon singled, Dick Groat walked and Bob Skinner got a tantalizing single over third base that Thomas wasn't up to and he'd lost another, 6–5.

Three years before it had been a different story. That July Craig had been called up from the St. Paul farm club by the Dodgers. They thought they had an outside chance for the pennant and needed help. He gave it to them, winning 11 games while losing only five. He was the pitching hero of the drive that won them the pennant.

In 1960 he was sidelined for two months with a broken collar-bone, but came back to win six straight Dodger games. He started the next season by beating the Reds and the Giants, but then began to get his lumps and fell into disfavor. By September he knew that his name would be on the list of expendables the Dodgers would offer the Mets and Houston in October.

Oh, there were happy days, although they didn't come around very often. Like the day Roger beat Milwaukee, winning one of those one-run games for a change, 6–5. It was a seven-hit, nine-inning job on June 20, the first time he was able to go the full distance in a winning effort.

Wins like that gave the Mets a lift—at that particular time of the season anyway.

"We know we don't have a good club," Craig said afterward, "but we always take the field thinking we can beat the other club.

"Losing gets you down, sure. You get tired of it. But

when the game's over I think to myself I'll be pitching again in three days or so. I forget about the bad game and start going over the batters I'll be pitching to next time out. I look ahead to a game I might win, the next one."

You seldom saw Roger sipping from a can of beer in evident enjoyment after a game or making with the jokes in the clubhouse. He had won 10 games and lost 24 in 1962. This time out he was to win only five while losing 22. And he was to suffer through another flock of one-run losses and games lost in the ninth or extra innings, not to mention the agonies of an 18-game losing streak.

Then one April night, he beat his old companions, the Los Angeles Dodgers, before 23,000 appreciative fans at the Polo Grounds, 4–2.

To Craig it was something to savor like old wine. He had never beaten the Dodgers before, although he insisted he had never pitched a poor game against them. He also insisted he held no resentment against the Los Angeles management for dropping him into the expansion draft pile.

"I talked to Duke Snider about it before the game," recalls Roger. "I mentioned how satisfying it would be to beat them. This win stands out in my mind as one of my biggest thrills, almost as big as the World Series game I won for Brooklyn against the Yankees in 1954."

There were a couple of run-producing balks committed, but they evened up, with both sides involved. This was a game at a time when the umpires were calling balks as though for exercise. Plate umpire Al Barlick called one on Craig as he was pitching to Bob Miller, the former Met, in the third. This brought home Ron Fairly with the second run of the inning and it loomed as a big run while Miller held onto that edge for six innings.

The Mets got to Miller for three runs in the seventh, however, with Ed Kranepool opening the rally with a double. Charley Neal bunted safely. Then Miller wild-pitched Kranepool home. Al Moran's single put Neal on third and Miller, who had won his first two starts as a Dodger, was taken out and Ed Roebuck called in from the bullpen. Roebuck's first act was to commit a balk while pitching to Marv' Throneberry, a pinch-hitter. This sent Neal across the plate with the run that made the score 3–2, and before the inning ended they added another.

By now the crowd was delirious. It was a joy to see the Dodgers get the short end of it. These same Dodgers who the year before had abused the maiden Mets so mercilessly, beating them in 16 out of 18 games and by such scores as 17–8, 13–6 and 17–3. In the upper left field stands fans hung a big sign reading:

"o'malley go home!"

"It was cold out there," said Casey Stengel. "But I love the cold, 'specially when we go ahead. The way the fans yelled we shoulda played a full day—a day shift an' a night shift, just to please them."

Craig had reason to believe it would be a different season after another early win, a 3–2 decision over the Cubs in Chicago. This was a day on which the Mets backed him up with something extra, for a change, in both hitting and fielding.

Frank Thomas slugged in the clutch this day, driving in a run in the first inning with a single and then breaking up a 1–1 tie with a two-run homer in the sixth.

In the field the team was superlative, the infielders putting together a pair of double-plays in a manner suggesting that they could do more of the same practically any old time. One was started by Craig himself by way of second baseman Ron Hunt and finally Gil Hodges. The second was an extra fancy affair that ended the game.

It happened when Lou Brock tried to go from first to third on an infield out. Charley Neal grabbed Ken Hubbs' grounder and threw him out. Hodges took the throw and was then surprised to see Brock trying for third. Not too surprised, though, to make a perfect throw to Al Moran, who had hustled over to cover for Neal, for the out.

A year before, it was agreed, something awful would have happened in a situation like that.

"Somebody—not Gil—would have thrown the ball away for sure," said Craig. "They'd have scored two runs and we'd have lost another. But this year you look around you and see an infield."

Craig liked the improvement in the club's catching too, he said. Norm Sherry, his roomie and old Dodger companion, had been the receiver.

"He's one of the greatest catchers I've ever seen," Craig said. "There's a reason for every pitch he calls. We don't have all those passed balls and wild pitches we had last year.

"Yes, this second year is different. The year before we used to figure that no matter how good things looked in the early innings, we'd find some way of losing before the end. This year we all figure we have a good chance of winning any day."

It didn't last, though. Soon he was on the losing side again, even in well-pitched games. When he lost a 4–3 game to the Dodgers at the Polo Grounds it was his and the Mets' twelfth in a row and a time for somber thoughts again.

"Going as bad as this," Craig remarked, "if you didn't know in your heart you were pitching well, you might feel like suicide. I try not to take the ball game home with me, the losing one, that is, but sometimes I can't help it. I know it hurts my wife too when she feels everything's going against me."

This was one of those almost-won-with-a-ninth-inning-rally affairs that seemed to be a frequent feature of the

Mets schedule. Don Drysdale had started, gone seven innings and then got out of there after Jesse Gonder had hit two homers and Duke Snider a single and a double. He let Ron Perranosky save it for him.

Rod Kanehl pinch-hit for Craig at the start of the ninth and singled. Jim Hickman followed with another hit which almost bounced over left fielder Tommy Davis' head. Davis had the spring in his legs to bring it down, and the inning ended with Tim Harkness taking a called third strike.

"When Kanehl got a hit in the ninth I thought maybe this would be one I'd win sitting on the bench," said Craig. "I thought Hickman might hit one out of sight."

In the middle of his long losing streak it seemed likely that this generous man might escape to another, better ball club. The Mets were in Cincinnati on the eve of the trading deadline and many reports had Craig going elsewhere. Some said it would be Milwaukee, others St. Louis and still others San Francisco or even back to the club that had shed him, the Dodgers. All four needed pitching help.

Craig waited far into the early morning hours for word that he had been dealt to one of the contenders, then decided he'd better get some sleep. The next day at breakfast the papers told him there had been no late trade developments on the Coast either. The escape hatch was closed.

"I didn't think I'd still be in this clubhouse today," he said on reporting for work at Crossley Field. "I thought I'd be traveling to another town.

"Deep down I thought they were asking too much for me to be able to make a trade. They wanted to get two for me—somebody who could play a position every day for them and a young pitcher to take my place."

After a particularly tough loss in Chicago, Craig had sat alone in the dugout for ten minutes after the game when usually he'd go to the clubhouse with the rest. Beaten again, he'd sit on his stool a while, having a one-handed wrestling match with a can of beer. After a decent interval the visitors would crowd around him and he'd answer all questions, however dumb or repetitious they might seem. He often displayed a dry humor in these post-mortem remarks.

Even in the midst of his incredibly long losing streak, his belief in the possibility of winning was renewed every fourth day.

"I try not to think about how many games I've lost," he said after dropping his seventeenth straight, 5–3, to the Dodgers in Los Angeles, "or think about how many I might lose. Sure, maybe I joke about it after a game, but I'll tell you this. If I ever find myself thinking about losing during a game I'll know it's time to quit."

There was bewildered sympathy for Craig again when he lost his eighteenth straight in Milwaukee on this most dreadful of road tours. It was one of the best games the Mets had played in some time and one in which they out-hit the opposition. But it ended in familiar fashion with the tying run on third base as a Mets batter took a third strike for the last out, the other fellows winning, 2–1.

The Mets got nine hits, six of them off Dan Schneider, a 20-year-old bonus pitcher, in the first five innings but couldn't put them together for a run. Twice Schneider got out of trouble with line drives at infielders that were turned into double plays.

"We hit maybe .215 all season like .215 hitters should," said Casey Stengel. "Now it's August an' we start hittin' some line drives an' what do we hit? Line drives for two outs!"

This was one of those games in which Craig helped beat himself. His first pitch to Eddie Mathews, the second batter in the first inning, resulted in that Brave belter's fifteenth home run of the season.

No pitcher has a better pick-off move than Craig, but when he used it this day it resulted in the Braves' winning run.

In the sixth inning, with the score still 1–1, he tried to catch Gene Oliver off first base for the second out with Lou Klimchock, another Milwaukee runner, pacing restlessly off third. Frank Thomas was the Mets' first baseman that day, which should have been a caution to Craig. Thomas played first base like a fellow who had been taking lessons from Marv' Throneberry.

Craig threw over three times. The third throw went into right field because Thomas' arm hit the runner as he went for the ball. As he chased it into the outfield Klimchock jogged home with the Braves' second run.

The only Mets hits that mattered came in the eighth inning, when Ron Hunt beat out an infield single and Jesse Gonder hit a scoring double to the right-field wall. In the ninth they staged one of their usual last-gasp rallies, but Bob Shaw came in from the bullpen and Joe Hicks looked at a called third strike for the third out with a Met runner at third base.

"If he bought a graveyard," commented Tracey Stallard, the country wit, "nobody would die."

His eighteenth straight put Roger in the record books. Only one other man in the history of the National League had lost as many as eighteen straight and you had to dig back to 1910 to learn that Clifton Curtis of the Boston Braves was the man.

Craig had one more to go before he matched the sad sack record of 19 in a row set by Johnny Nabors, of the old Philadelphia Athletics, in 1916. He lost his nineteenth in the second game of a double-header against the Boston

Red Sox. Tom Sheehan, the Giants' scout, who had lost the first game, 1–0, remembers the day. Nabors was winning 1–0 going into the home half of the ninth inning.

"Nabors got the first man out," he said. "Then Whitey Witt, an outfielder who was playing short for us that day, booted one. The next guy walked. Harry Hopper was next. He singled and the runner tried to score from second. Our left fielder whips one in that has the runner by 15 feet.

"But we have a green catcher, the ball bounces out of his glove, the runner scores, the other guy takes third and it's a one-one ball game.

"Nabors winds up and throws the next one 20 feet over the batter's head. The man on third walked home and we lost, two to one.

"I asked Johnny what happened on that pitch. 'Listen you,' he yelled, 'I knew, an' so did everybody else, that those bums playin' for us couldn't get me another run if we played all week. If you think I'm going to throw nine more innings out there on a hot day like this you're crazy.' "

Craig was the Mets' player representative, an indication of what his teammates thought of him. This August night at the Polo Grounds he called an early pre-game meeting to discuss grievances, pension plan payments and other business.

"Well, that's it," he said to them at the close. "No, there's one thing more. I'd really like to win this one to-night, boys."

They did it. They beat the Cubs for him, seven to three. His epic streak was over after 18 straight defeats.

The game for a long while had all the earmarks of many others lost along the way since he had last won a game on April 29, a 4–2 decision over the Dodgers. He got a lead, then blew it, and went into the ninth in a familiar setting, the score tied, 3–3.

Nothing happened, however, in the Cub half and then the Mets came up. Frank Thomas was an out, but Joe Hicks singled. Choo Choo Coleman struck out, but Al Moran doubled. Lindy McDaniel came out of the bullpen for the Cubs to replace Paul Toth. The first thing he did was to walk Tim Harkness, batting for Craig. Jim Hickman was at three balls and two strikes when he hit a fly ball to left. It just ticked the overhang of the upper stands before falling to the field. On the dugout steps Casey took off his cap and waved it in a grand slam circle. The 11,000 fans sounded like a dozen times that many.

Craig bolted for the plate so fast he beat Hicks, jogging in from third as the first man in the most wonderful parade Craig had ever seen. Al Forman, the plate umpire, had to hold him back so that he could see that Hicks stepped on home plate. When Hickman arrived Roger gave him a bear hug.

They had tried all sorts of things to help Craig's luck change. Norm Sherry had sought a black cat without success. He had planned to have Roger carry it out to the box with him before making his first pitch. Roger had changed the number on his back from "38" to "13" at the suggestion of Ted Decker, the clubhouse guard, who told him he had a dream in which he saw Roger winning a game with "13" on his shirt.

There were six defeats that were lost by a single run in his 18-game streak, and the toughest perhaps was the one he lost 2–1 in Philadelphia, his fourteenth:

He was actually winning a 1–0 game going into the ninth. Then, with one out, he made two bad pitches. Tony Gonzales hit the first for a two-bagger. Roy Seivers hit the second for a winning, two-run homer.

It was almost as bad, same park, same situation, a few weeks later. Grover Powell had shut the Phils out, 4–0 in the first game. Craig was two strikes away from a 1–0 decision and the Mets first double shut-out, when he fed Seivers a fat pitch on a two-ball, one-strike count and saw it lined into the left field stands for a tying homer. The game was lost in the tenth inning by Larry Bearnarth, who had taken over.

Came a later night in Philadelphia and Craig's turn to pitch.

"If we're ahead in the ninth an' Seivers is coming up to hit," said Casey Stengel on the way out to the ball yard, "I'm gonna get the hell out of that park an' I'm gonna take Craig with me!"

Well, in the ninth, with the Mets leading 6–1, Johnny Callison singled and Wes Covington doubled. An outfield fly brought in one run and up stepped Seivers, the villain who had ruined him twice before. In the press rookery they waited to see Stengel rush from the dugout with a butterfly net to capture his pitcher and lead him away but nothing of the sort happened. Craig pitched—and Seivers grounded out. Clay Dalrymple singled but Craig handled Don Hoak's roller himself for the third out.

Craig, who must have a Pollyanna concealed in his genealogical table, was again sure that he would be traded.

He went home to Lakewood, Calif., to wait as patiently as he had in game after game for some strong measures in his behalf by the supporting cast. On November 4 it came, the news that he had been traded to the St. Louis Cardinals for Outfielder George Altman and Bill Wakefield, a young pitcher.

No prisoner ever received a pardon with more sincere expressions of gratitude.

"My two seasons with the Mets were a blessing," said Roger. "It taught me how to cope with adversity."

BIG KIDS

There will doubtless be many big weeks in Edward E. Kranepool's life, but the week of June 24, 1962, will do as a starter. On Tuesday of that week the 6'3", 205-pound good-looking youngster graduated from James Monroe High School in New York's Bronx. On Wednesday he signed with the Mets for a spaced bonus of about $80,000, and on Friday he took his first plane ride to join the club in Los Angeles. On Saturday he worked out with them there and was the object of much attention by the sportswriters, broadcasters and cameramen.

Getting on the players bus to report to the hotel in downtown Los Angeles afterwards he was besieged by youngsters seeking autographs while such Mets players as Gil Hodges, Roger Craig and Marv' Throneberry stood by unasked.

At James Monroe, Ed Kranepool, as a sophomore first baseman, hit .492 and broke Hank Greenberg's schoolboy home-run record by belting nine home runs. He was co-captain of the team. He also played basketball, averaging 29.5 points a game.

By the time he was a senior, the major league scouts were flocking to James Monroe games and to the Kranepool home. The Chicago White Sox, Detroit Tigers and San Francisco Giants were particularly hot after him. Willard Marshall, the old Giant outfielder, had sent in a highly complimentary report on the boy to his old club.

Kranepool went to a Mets tryout at the Polo Grounds at the invitation of Bubber Jonnard, their metropolitan district scout. He hit nine balls into the right field stands and Johnny Murphy decided that here was a youth worth a good hunk of Mrs. Payson's money.

His mother had supported him ever since his father, whom he never saw, was killed in World War II. She had often driven Eddie to ball games.

"We were Giant fans before they left New York," said Mrs. Ethel Kranepool, "and when they compare Eddie to Mel Ott it's a great compliment."

Murphy and Jonnard went to the Kranepool home soon after the day he had bombed the right field seats during his tryout. They arrived at eight o'clock at night and said they wouldn't leave until he had signed with the Mets.

"We talked and talked until it was almost midnight," Mrs. Kranepool recalled. "Then Mr. Murphy looked at Eddie and said, 'Tell me, how much do you think you're worth?'

"Eddie looked at me for help, but I told him it was his decision to make. And do you know he came out with the exact figure I would have given them."

But more than a big bonus bundle entered into the youngster's decision to go with the Mets.

"I knew I'd have a bigger opportunity with them than with clubs that already had established men at every position," he says today. "I'd also have a faster opportunity. Besides I wanted to play with my hometown team. And where do you get bigger recognition than in New York?"

The Mets farmed him out to Syracuse, their top farm

club and he hit .229 in 17 games. Then they shifted him to Knoxville, where he hit .278, and finally to Auburn, of the Pony League, trying to find the right level. Auburn was the answer. In 20 games he hit .351.

The following spring they had him in the winter rookie league, something that grew from an idea started by Casey Stengel in his early Yankee years to speed up the development of young players. Then they moved him into the regular training camp at St. Petersburg. He had quite a spring. Playing first base in the final game of the exhibition schedule at Portsmouth, Virginia, he slugged three home runs in the Mets 7–2 victory over Baltimore.

"They tell me, why you can't play that boy, he's only 18 years old," Casey was saying after the club landed in New York. "I say what's the matter with being 18? Mel Ott was a big leaguer when *he* was 18. So was Fred Lindstrom. And so was Bobby Feller.

"You know I haven't seen him swing at a bad pitch yet. He has a good left-handed swing and he doesn't go chasing after those bad pitches. That's more than I can say for most of my other players.

"I couldn't play him on any other club, but here he can make it because we always got the shorts. Why I saw him start a double-play one day when he was the first baseman an' he surprised me. He can play that base. Oops, I said to myself, I'd better shut my mouth."

Casey put him into the line-up as an outfielder on opening day. It wasn't much of an opening and neither were a number of games after that, but when the Mets broke through for their first victory, over Milwaukee, 4–3, on April 19, Kranepool's contribution was his first major league home run.

He surprised a lot of people, including the Phillies, in a later game at the Polo Grounds when he won a game outright for them for the first time.

With runners on first and second and two out in the

ninth, Eddie watched Jack Baldschun, the Phils' top relief jobber, throw three straight balls. He looked down to Cookie Lavagetto, coaching at third base, for the sign.

Lavagetto flashed him the hit sign if, of course, he thought the pitch was good. Baldschun threw and Tony Vinzon, the plate umpire, called it a strike. Then, on the next, the three-and-one pitch, he looped a double into right field to score the winning run.

"I asked the kid later an' he told me he thought the ball was a little outside," said Stengel. "I said, 'Oh, is that so, but the umpire didn't think so.' But this kid just won't swing unless he thinks it's a strike. It takes some men years to learn the strike zone. An' some of them never learn it."

Earlier in that important time at bat, this fuzz-cheeked phenom' Kranepool, who had looked at the last pitch suspiciously, asked Umpire Vinson to look at the ball. The count was two balls, no strikes.

"It looked smudged to me," he said afterward. "That gives a screwball pitcher like Baldschun an edge." But the ump' kept it in play.

Most young hitters would never have thought of checking the ball. Or, if they had, wouldn't have had the nerve to make the request. But Kranepool did.

"This kid," the manager said, "I expected him to have trouble, but he was one of the few who hasn't had it. He stands up to a pitcher good an' he's been good in the field wherever I play him. In the outfield I've seen him play a carom off the wall good and throw home to keep a man from scorin'. An' like in that first game I expected him to be nervous, but he wasn't an' he didn't strike out. I've seen much older men strike out three times in their first game."

Through talking about Kranepool, Casey picked up his towel and plodded toward the showers.

"Youth!" he shouted over his shoulder. "The youth of America!"

Eddie had used some of his bonus money to buy his mother a split-level house in White Plains, and he bought a white Thunderbird to take him to and from the Polo Grounds, among other things.

He was a pretty hot hitter, the favorite of the fans. For a while he batted around the .300 mark.

"Hittin's the best point he's got right now," said Stengel. "He amazes you. He stands up at that plate as though he's been there four or five years. The pitchers are readin' him extra careful, but so far they haven't caught on as much as he has."

After 40 games, however, the youngster's batting average was down to .225. That was about par for the Mets, of course, but they were worried that continued mistreatment might damage his confidence.

The left-handers bothered him most, of course, and the Mets, with such left-handed hitters as Duke Snider, Tim Harkness and others, had a lot of lefties lined up against them.

"They're really working on me," Kranepool said one day." Both right-handers and left-handers. They know more about me than they did earlier. I didn't see many left-handers in high school, of course, and anyway that's just high school pitching.

"But I didn't get to bat against much left-handed pitching in spring training, either. It takes time to get used to them. The more I see of them the faster I should learn."

The management, though, thought he might well be ruined if he were thrown in there against major league pitching much longer. And the experience he needed couldn't be won as a bench warmer or occasional pinch-hitter. It wasn't long after old pro Curt Simmons, a left-hander, had fanned him four straight times, that they decided to farm him out to Buffalo. He was hitting .206.

He came back September 4 at St. Louis, a day late because he had missed the plane on which they had reserved space for him in New York, and talking of the $56 he said they owed him because he had to buy another ticket himself.

He also came back talking like a boy who thought minor league life was for the birds. He had sampled big league luxuries. In spite of strange hours and day games following night games and cross-country flights at all hours, it was still, after all, the big time.

"At Buffalo about all I did was play at night and sleep all day," he said. "The International League is an endurance league. I was tired all the time. I don't like it in the minors at all."

He made four singles his first day back on the job, as the Cardinals beat the Mets, six to five. The first three were off Ernie Broglio and the fourth off old teammate Ken McKenzie, a left-hander.

"He still looks good to me," said Casey Stengel. "He still hits the ball up the middle."

"I like him," said Johnny Keane, manager of the Cardinals. "Any kid just 18 years old who can stand up there and face major league pitching like he does has got to be good. Home runs? You know it was some time before Musial hit homers regularly. It takes time for a player to learn how to use his hands and get the most out of his body and his power."

They talked mostly about power at the Polo Grounds, where it meant so much. Cookie Lavagetto, watching him hit in practice there one night, was impressed with his level swing and his knowledge of the strike zone.

"He looks like he's going to be a good hitter for average," Lavagetto said. "Whether he'll hit for power I don't know, but he looks like a .320 hitter. Is that bad?"

His manager said he wanted to see him keep hitting up the middle.

"You couldn't pull the ball on high school pitchers," he shouted one night in sheer exasperation. "What makes you think you can pull major league hitters?

"Let him hit to center," continued Casey. "There was another fellow played at the Polo Grounds who couldn't pull the ball either. He just hit it center and left center an' hit it so good he hit .400 one year and way up near there all the other years. Fellow by the name of Bill Terry."

Another infant Met who caused Casey Stengel to begin his post-game orations with a cheer for the youth of America, was Larry Bearnarth, a husky blond who became an effective relief pitcher at the age of 22 and with only one-half a season of minor league ball behind him.

Bearnarth, a Long Island youngster, was a minor phenomenon with St. John's University, losing only two games in his entire college career. The Mets got him for a $25,000 bonus and started him off with their Syracuse farm club in the summer of 1961.

"When I won my first two games I thought I had it made," he said. "I thought they'd be calling me back to New York in no time at all."

He stayed to lose 13 games, finish with a 2–13 record and return home a very disheartened young pitcher.

"The worst of it was I got my lumps in the early innings in 12 straight games," he said, "and it got so I thought I'd never get anybody out."

However, that winter he pitched for the Mets' St. Petersburg team in the Florida Instructional League under Solly Hemus. He worked hard, learned a lot and moved into the regular training camp with renewed confidence. Sid Hudson, the old Washington pitcher, had helped him improve his sinker and he taught himself a change-of-pace pitch. He earned the trip north by not allowing an earned run in the exhibition games.

The first pitching he did for the Mets was against the

Reds in Cincinnati. He said he felt a little nervous, particularly when he was pitching to Frank Robinson.

"He got two hits off me," said Larry. "I decided right there it wouldn't pay to get nervous any more."

He didn't, either. Casey Stengel, frequently shocked by the sight of relief pitchers coming in from the bullpen with their knees knocking, admired his nerve. He began to call upon the youngster more frequently.

The Bearnarth boy responded with four innings of shutout pitching against the Giants. Later he pitched five more of the same against the power-packed club.

"He's no Ned in the Third Reader," said Casey, enthusing over a job the youngster had turned in on the Giants. "When the pitchin' coach says somethin', he listens. Then he executes.

"Did you see how he had Willie Mays lungin' like a rookie on that change-of-pace pitch?" Casey went on, "a beauty!

"He hasn't a lot of pitches but he has control of what he has. He might be the man I can put in in the seventh, eighth or ninth innin' with confidence. An' lemme tell you somethin' else he's learned. He's learned you can't let them big hitters dig in on you or crowd the plate. He's learned it sometimes pays to be tough."

Came a wild game with the Reds at the Polo Grounds in which Bearnarth was touched for successive doubles to cut the Mets' lead to 13–12. Frank Robinson, whom Bearnarth remembered from his first game, was the next batter.

Robinson was hit by a pitch into his ribs. The next two Reds, properly impressed, or anyway careful, struck out.

Casey, who had been unable to convince some of his other pitchers, particularly Jay Hook, that it paid to disturb the batters, chuckled in the dugout.

FAREWELL POLO GROUNDS

Had anyone at Ebbets Field, the bilious blue home of the old Brooklyn Dodgers, ever said that sometime, somehow there would be a Duke Snider Night at the Polo Grounds, he would have been carted off to the looney bin. But then what fan before 1957 would have believed that a man named O'Malley, whose roots are in Brooklyn, would move the Dodgers to California, or that Brooklyn's beloved Duke would eventually wind up, old and gray, on another new New York club?

But there he was, on the night of Friday, the 13th of September, standing at home plate with a mobile golf cart, the gift of his Met teammates, and other handsome gifts; with Carl Furillo, Roy Campanella, Jackie Robinson and other old Brooklyn teammates, friends and relatives around him.

The San Francisco Giants, with Willie Mays starring, won the ball game, but it still seemed a Snider holiday to most of the 27,000 present.

The Duke made a speech. "I really don't know what to

say," he began. "I look up into the stands and it looks like
Ebbets Field. The Mets are wonderful but you can't take
the Dodgers out of Brooklyn."

The roar of the crowd indicated that there were many
former inhabitants of Ebbets Field in the house and that
they appreciated his allegiance to them. They remembered his many great years there.

Snider's acquisition was a full-scale soap opera production that took up several weeks of the springtime. Would
Snider come to the Mets? Would the Yankees get him instead? Was Stengel wary because of Duke's bad knee?
Would Snider's big salary kill the deal? Day after day this
suspense story ran. With the co-operation of Buzzy Bavasi,
the Dodgers' general manager, they managed to milk more
newspaper space than Liz Taylor. The mail poured in,
most of it in favor of his purchase.

When all was said and done the money—an estimated
$30,000 at the time, plus the veteran's $38,000 salary—was
worth it. Snider lent the class of an old pro to the club, he
undoubtedly drew people in the gate and he helped the
Mets win ball games.

He hit only .257 and that bothered him. So did that
tired feeling in his 36-year-old legs, the rolls of fat on his
stomach and the dog days of August. But he was in 129
ball games during the season, compared to the limited
service he had seen with the Dodgers the season before.
And last place or not, a lot of it had been fun.

He hit 14 homers for the Mets. The first of them off
Warren Spahn, of the Braves, was his first hit as a Met.

There was the game with the Cardinals that Al Jackson
seemed about to lose 2–0, after a lot of gallant pitching.
The Mets, hitting only .206 as a team, had managed to get
only two hits up to the ninth off Ron Taylor. Then Frank
Thomas singled and Ron Hunt drew a base on balls. Up

came Snider, and out of the game came Taylor, three-hitter and all. After all, the Duke had a career total at the moment of 398 home runs.

Manager Johnny Keane called Diomedes Olivo, a left-hander, out of the bullpen. The new pitcher ran the count to two strikes and a ball. His catcher, Gene Oliver, missed the second strike and the runners each moved up a base.

That left first base open but the Cards declined to put Snider, the potential winning run, on base. Olivo pitched another ball and then Snider fouled one off. The Cards, who had been holding one conference after another in the pitcher's box, called another. When it was over, Olivo made his three-and-two pitch, and the Duke slammed it on a line into the right field seats for the ball game, 3–2.

"I notice they didn't have any huddle on the mound after Snider hit it," said a happy Stengel afterwards. "The funny thing about all those huddles is that they tell me that pitcher can't understand English. All those infielders and outfielders an' the manager were just talkin' to each other an' he was the one who had to make the pitch."

"I've learned more baseball from Casey Stengel this season," said Snider at a luncheon on Long Island prior to his Night at the Polo Grounds, "than I had under all my other managers in my 15 years in the majors.

"I try to sit near him on the bench and talk to him. It helps me. All my life I've tried to figure out the moves in different situations as they arise and then see how the manager does it. It's unbelievable what clever answers Casey comes up with.

"I always used to kid him when we played against the Yankees in the World Series but I don't think I realized then what a sound baseball man he is. And he's great with the young players because he likes to inject some humor into the game.

"The man is a marvel at handling players, in talking to

them. And he sits up all night, talks to anybody he sees, gets mad if you quit on him to go to bed and is probably the first one on the bus for the ball park that next morning. I've never seen such an amazing man."

Although at the close of the first season motor boats had been presented to Mets Marv' Throneberry and Richie Ashburn, both of whom turned out to live in completely landlocked parts of the country, the Howard Clothes people who made the awards resolved to solve the problem the next time out. When Ron Hunt, the 22-year-old second baseman, was voted the most valuable Met by the fans, they wheeled out a $4,000 Acqua-Car, able and willing to go by land or by water.

In Hunt's case it really didn't matter. He lives in a suburb of St. Louis where he could drive it from his home down to the Mississippi and cruise away.

"He broke it in right," relates Joe McDonald, of the Mets. "After the game he drove it to the foot of Dyckman Street and took it into the water. He drove it across the Hudson River and then drove it up the Palisades to the place where he lives in Fort Lee. Saved the George Washington Bridge toll."

Hunt was a $20,000 bonus baby with Milwaukee. He started as a third baseman, but when the Braves saw that Red Schoendienst was through, the farm clubs were told to concentrate on the development of a second baseman. He was on their Austin farm in the Texas League and hitting .311 when Solly Hemus, one of Stengel's coaches, was sent to watch him. Hemus recommended him lavishly; the Mets purchased him conditionally.

There were half a dozen second-base candidates at St. Petersburg, including Larry Burright, the former Dodger, and Ted Schreiber, the Mets' number one draft choice, but Hunt beat them all out.

The Mets had until May 9, the day the roster had to be

cut, to complete the deal but Hunt made them make up their minds before that:

Going into the home half of the ninth inning, they were trailing Milwaukee, 4–3, and on the verge of losing their ninth straight game. With two out, Hunt doubled in two runs for the first Mets victory in 1962. That night a florist delivered flowers to Ron's wife, a present from a happy Mets owner, Mrs. Joan Payson.

A well-packed 186-pounder, Hunt wasn't always as healthy as he looked. He suffered from hay fever, asthma, a variety of allergies and had a locker loaded with pills of all colors and sizes. He also had cuts and scars all over his legs, souvenirs from infielders in retaliation for his hard-nosed manner of trying to break up double-plays. If he seemed to wear the dirtiest uniform in the league it was with good reason. Many a time he would go into first base with a headlong slide, something old Polo Grounds fans hadn't seen since Frankie Frisch was the Giants' second baseman.

On the club's first road trip, Hunt helped develop a winning rally against Houston by bunting with two strikes against him. A week later in Los Angeles he shocked the Dodgers by stealing home.

"He made our infield," said Casey. "He settled the second base situation for me. My shortstop Moran became a changed ball player once Hunt started to work with him. He didn't have to worry as much over goin' to his left because he knew Hunt would cover the ground.

"Hunt's a major leaguer," continued Casey. "He hits the low pitches, he can hit to right an' he knows how to execute the hit an' run. What you got to like is that he can do all those things against the good pitchers. They don't scare him."

In mid-season Hunt, plagued by the virus, had complained of fatigue. But he finished strongest of all the

Mets. He hit safely in 13 of the last 14 games at a .452 pace. He finished with more base-hits than any other Met. Pete Rose, of Cincinnati, was voted the National League Rookie of the Year, but Hunt was a strong second. He was the only rookie besides Rose who got first-place votes.

Tom Tresh and Al Moran were the names of two high school wonders in the Detroit area in 1958. Major league scouts haunted their games and their homes, offering them all sorts of extravagant inducements.

The Yankees offered Moran $60,000 to sign a contract. The Boston Red Sox offered him $50,000. The young man chose the Red Sox.

"The Yankees had Tony Kubek at shortstop," explains Moran. "Kubek's a young man. I just figured he'd be their shortstop for more years than I could wait. I didn't want to spend that many years on their farm clubs in the minors. The Red Sox had Don Buddin. So I went for the better opportunity."

Boston sent Moran to its Memphis farm and his first night on the job he got five hits in five times at bat. He wondered how many days it would be before they called him back to Boston. While he was wondering his batting average dropped. They moved him to Allentown and other places. In Boston they wrote him off as $50,000 more of Tom Yawkey's misspent money.

When the Mets and Red Sox talked trade at the winter meetings, Boston asked for Felix (Wrong Way) Mantilla. In exchange they offered Pumpsie Green, the famous traveler, and Tracy Stallard, a Lil' Abner type known principally as the pitcher who had tossed the ball that Roger Maris had clobbered for his record 61st home run. The Mets asked them to throw in one more player.

"How about that shortstop, Moran?" asked Johnny Murphy who had been the Red Sox farm director. "We'd like him for our Buffalo farm club."

Moran did not report to Buffalo that spring; he did so well at St. Pete the manager gave him the shortstop job. But in July, when his average was below .200, they shipped him to Buffalo and tried Burright at short.

"I know I haven't hit," Moran moaned at the time, "But I also know no one in the National League has played a better shortstop."

The Mets found that out and recalled him, but at season's end his average was .193. Still and all, he had plenty of company in that neighborhood, for nine Mets batted .200 or lower.

Said Cookie Lavagetto, "Moran has a lot of guts. If he and Coleman could learn to hit they'd own the world."

One day Casey Stengel was suffering from the pitching shorts, his chronic complaint, before a particular doubleheader in Philadelphia even started. Roger Craig, ever willing, volunteered to work one game. Ernie White, the pitching coach, scorning the names of overworked bullpen laborers, came up with a new one, "Grover David Demetrius Powell."

"Where'd you pull that one from," a historian of the Mets asked, "out of your hat?"

"Practically," said Ernie. "I know the kid's never started a game before, but he's looked good in the few relief turns he did. He might surprise 'em."

The 22-year-old youngster did just that, slamming a four-hit shutout at the Phils to win 4–0.

"How about that!" shouted Stengel in the clubhouse afterward. "How about that for a 14-year-old boy? Jus' wait until he gets to be 16 an' has all his strength from eatin' all that breakfast cereal an' so on an' so forth.

"You know he was such a brilliant fella because he went to that big university down the street which he got throwed off the team an' that gave us a chance to sign him. Now if some other big universities throw some more young fellas like him off their teams an' we can beat the other scouts to signin' 'em. . . ."

Powell had pitched in parts of nine games after being called up from the Raleigh farm club in the Carolina League. He had been wild in most of them. Now, after retiring the lead-off man, Tony Taylor, he walked Johnny Callison and Tony Gonzales. Then the kid got Don Demeter on a pop fly and struck out Don Hoak.

In the sixth, while they were still waiting for him to collapse, he walked Roy Seivers and Demeter with two out, and Hoak followed with a scratch hit. This time he was out of it on Clay Dalrymple's grounder to Ron Hunt.

All the while he had been matching zeros on the scoreboard with Cal McLish. Powell was rewarded, finally, in the eighth when the Mets scored twice on singles by Al Moran, Powell's own bunt, a single by Jim Hickman and a double by Tim Harkness. The Mets added two more in the ninth.

Powell had attended the University of Pennsylvania's Wharton School of Business. In his sophomore season he led the country's college pitchers in strikeouts. In his junior year he was kicked off the squad.

"We had a game scheduled with Army at West Point," he explains. "We also had a tough exam coming up, so I stayed up cramming until six o'clock in the morning. The bus left at 7:30 and I never made it. They cut me from the squad."

The Mets signed him for $2,500 in the spring of 1961, $1,000 down and the rest to be paid if he stayed in the organization ninety days. He went to Syracuse and compiled a 6–2 record, then to Auburn where he did likewise. He was 5–6 at Raleigh when the Mets yelled for him to come and get it.

In September Elijah "Pumpsie" Green, who had been sentenced to their Buffalo farm club in the spring, rejoined the Mets in Cincinnati. This surprised a number of people, for it was only one day after he had left Buffalo. Pumpsie had often had trouble with time and travel.

Once he and Gene Conley, the pitcher, were with the Boston Red Sox. After leaving Yankee Stadium the bus carrying the club had stalled on the approaches to the George Washington Bridge. Conley and Green sat still for a while, then Conley said nuts to this, he was going to the restaurant back in the bus station. Pumpsie said me too and didn't get to Washington until the next night, waking up the following morning to learn he'd been hit with a heavy fine.

"I was only gone a day," he protested.

But here was Pumpsie, the new Pumpsie. On schedule and 26 pounds lighter than in spring training.

"I got all that hog fat I had this spring from sittin' around waitin' to play for the Red Sox," he said. "In Buffalo I ran a lot an' didn't eat so much. You can't eat much on International League meal money anyway."

In Cincinnati he got five hits in his first seven times at bat. In Cincinnati they flash the batter's average on the scoreboard when he steps to the plate. It can be embarrassing, as in the case of the Mets' catcher, Norm Sherry, for example, who at one point was hitting .097. But when Pumpsie batted for the first time the next night, there for all the people in Crosley Field to see was, "Green—.714."

"Almost the first thing people do is ask me how I got my nickname," says Pumpsie. "I figure eight million people have asked me so far, almost half of them sportswriters. When I get out of baseball I'm gonna' write a book entitled, 'How I Got the Name of Pumpsie' and sell a million copies at a dollar apiece."

The maiden Mets played what they thought at the time

was their last game at the Polo Grounds on Sunday, September 23. It turned out that the wake was premature, for their new stadium was still being built at the speed of an ant hill, and they were destined to do business at the same old stand in 1963.

The nostalgia of the occasion even affected Jack E. Lee, the public address system orator who doubled as the park disc jockey. As the innings ticked away he played such oldies as "This Old House" and "Auld Lang Syne."

"It took the Giants 50 years to leave the Polo Grounds for dead," said one oldtimer, "but the Mets buried it twice in two years."

Anyway, they beat the Chicago Cubs that day in the ninth, 2 to 1. Bob (The Right) Miller, who had last pitched a complete game three years before, started, and when the Chicagos leaped to a one-run lead in the first inning on two bases on balls, a wild pitch and a single, it seemed a sure thing that he would add another loss to his 0–12 record.

Miller settled down, however, and proceeded to pitch brilliant ball. When he left for a pinch-hitter in the eighth, he had given up only one more hit and one more walk and struck out nine.

It was a day mixed with hope for the future too, as in the eighth, Ed Kranepool, the 17-year-old high school bonus infant, got his first hit, a double sliced down the left-field foul line. When the next two batters walked, Casey Stengel sent Marvelous Marv' Throneberry up to pinch-hit. The Cubs called for a left-handed relief pitcher. The manager beckoned Marvelous back and asked Felix Mantilla to bat instead. Mantilla fouled out, and Gil Hodges, batting for Miller, struck out.

They managed to finish with a flourish, however, when they got another chance in the ninth. Choo Choo Coleman dropped a two-bagger into right field and went to third on a wild pitch. Frank Thomas then cashed him with the winning run by hitting a single.

They staged a television broadcast at home plate after the game. The camera panned around the old park as Lindsay Nelson gave its history. Then Casey, as usual, took over.

"You'd have to say this is a park with treee-mendous memories for me," he agreed. "I played here for John McGraw an' I played here against him, an' I batted here against pitchers like Christy Mathewson.

"They may tear it down, if they ever get around to it, which you never know, but they'll always talk about it. Years from now the newspaper fellas will come up to that young fella Kranepool, an' say, 'Did you ever play in the Polo Grounds, Mr. Kranepool?'

" 'Indeed I did,' he'll say. 'Why I made my first major league hit at the Polo Grounds!'

"Before I go to the clubhouse, I'd like to say I appreciate the job you fellas did here telecastin' our games here for Ballantine beer. I thank you."

"Say, Case'," someone called to him afterward in the clubhouse, "you pulled a boner. It's Rheingold, not Ballantine, that sponsors the telecasts."

"Holy smoke," exclaimed Casey, "I'll lose my job!"

HELLO SHEA STADIUM

Came the Spring of '65; as the Mets went into the fourth glorious year of their existence the list of originals had dwindled. The last to feel the wrench of leaving the old school and its glorious traditions was Rod Kanehl, who was assigned to their Buffalo farm club.

This left only Al Jackson and Jim Hickman of the only, the original Mets. There were others who were around that first spring in St. Petersburg, including Joe Christopher and Chris Cannizzaro, but only Jackson and Hickman lived through all three seasons.

Choo Choo Coleman, Elio Chacon, Ray Daviault, Ed Bouchee and others shuffled off to Buffalo long before Kanehl. Duke Snider escaped to the Giants. Gene Woodling became one of Hank Bauer's coaches with the Baltimore Orioles. Roger Craig, traded to the Cardinals, later moved on to the Cincinnati Reds in another deal. Jay Hook, shipped to Milwaukee in the deal for Roy McMillan, was dropped to the Braves' farm club. Don Zimmer moved to the Cincinnati Reds and then to the Washington Senators, where his manager was Gil Hodges, once a sainted Met.

Richie Ashburn spoke of his old club lovingly now from his seat in a radio and TV rookery for a Philadelphia station. Marv' Throneberry decided that he had enough of life as a Buffalo Bison and went home, buried his spiked shoes and old Met uniform in the back yard and became a Memphis beer salesman.

Some found it hard to leave town even when the Mets moved them to another club. Tracey Stallard, a bachelor out of no less a municipality than Herald, Virginia, shared a New York apartment with Phil Linz, of the Yankees, during the 1964 season. While one was away the other was home to play.

When the baseball journalists found the two bachelors were staying in town for the off-season, it was decided to put them to work in the annual Baseball Writers of America New York Chapter show at the Hotel Americana late in January, 1965. Along with Yankees Jim Bouton and Joe Pepitone they were supplied with way-out outfits, wigs, kazoos, washboards, banjos and other instruments. The leader of baseball's version of the Beatles, naturally, was harmonica-playing Phil Linz.

With hardly any trouble at all, the Mets finished last in the National League again in 1964. They did manage to win 53 games, however, two more than ever before by upending the St. Louis Cardinals, of all people, twice in the three tingling days that closed the season.

"If they make the season long enough," said Casey Stengel when all was said and done, "we'll pick up all the marbles yet."

Even so they were more popular losers than ever, thanks to a still-growing clientele and the handsome new ball yard in which they could entertain, in their inimitable fashion, the paying guests.

Splendiferous Shea Stadium opened to a crowd of 50,132 customers and went on from there, the turnstiles humming like crazy. When the season closed the Mets had drawn 1,732,597 at home, second in baseball only to the Los Angeles Dodgers. They outdrew the champion New York Yankees, who led the American League in home attendance, by 426,959. This despite the latter's belated recognition of the threat to their box-office domination of the New York baseball scene as manifested by a shakewell operation in management and such schemes as attempting to woo the friendship of the town's taxi pilots with free seats and starting some games at six o'clock in an effort to attract suburbanites.

Only three major league clubs played to audiences of better than 50,000 and the Mets did this five times. The Dodgers had six such turnouts, the Yankees two. Shea also bulged with crowds not registered in League attendance tables, such as the 50,850 who watched the 1964 All Star hootenanny and the 55,396 present for the annual Mayor's Trophy benefit game with the Yankees.

Undoubtedly the fact that many wanted to see the Mets' new playpen had something to do with the soar in attendance. So did the stadium's proximity to the World's Fair. There were days and nights, in fact, when the Fair people blamed the fun show at Shea for attendance falling below that expected on their own acres. Shea, lit up or merely sunbathed, was a sight rivaling all the Fair exhibits and attracted many a side visit from strangers from Peoria to Outer Mongolia who wanted to see for themselves if it was true what they said about Casey Stengel and his off-Broadway avant-garde performers.

Built on Flushing Meadows, a section of metropolitan New York where they once dumped garbage, and not far from where Gypsy Rose Lee, the stately stripper, was hailed as Queen of the Midway at a previous World's Fair, the new home of the Mets was so long going up people thought the constructors must be using the same timetable as the fellows who built the Pyramids.

It had been hoped that the Mets would be able to start their second, or 1963 season, at Shea, named after the man who had done so much to bring the National League back to New York. Construction problems, however, bad weather, labor difficulties and maybe a shortage of erasers and pencils or something in the planning office, prevented this. Although construction was speeded up it wasn't even ready for the Jets, New York's entry in the American Football League, to use that fall either. Shea Stadium figured to have the most delayed opening since King Tut's tomb.

When it was finally ready the citizens could hardly wait to buy their way in. The Mets drew some 140,000 in their first three home games, over 75,000 more than had paid to see their first three games at the crummy old Polo Grounds the year before.

The first nine games at Shea drew 238,532, almost a quarter of the 1,080,108 who saw them at home the season before. Moreover they had, in that earlier stretch, played the Giants three times and the Dodgers once. In their first nine at Shea in 1964 they played only against the Pittsburgh Pirates, St. Louis Cardinals, Cincinnati Reds and Chicago Cubs.

The games later with the Giants and Dodgers were the ones that set Joe DeGregorio, the comptroller of the club, to purring happily. They played to 357,475 against the Giants and 326,231 with the Dodgers. Visiting secretaries always brought along extra money bags to Shea in order to be able to cart home the guest club's share of the gate receipts. Visiting the Mets at home was like dropping into the U.S. Mint.

The Harry M. Stevens firm, whose founder set up the first peanut, hot dog and cold drink stand at the old Polo Grounds, had lost the concession franchise at Yankee Stadium after many years. The Stevens people could laugh it off, however, as they busied themselves at the many attractive food and drink stations at Shea, as well as the extra-special Diamond Club for season box-holders, with its own escalator, bar and restaurant.

The fans weren't the only ones who found themselves pleased with the stadium that was so long in coming. The players were pampered with such things as wall-to-wall carpeting in their recovery rooms, lounges in which they could view themselves or other performers doing shaving commercials on TV and dugouts so big they could almost hide from the manager. The coaches had a room of their own, the managers likewise. The umpires, asked to dress in rooms that amounted to little more than closets in other parks, were not neglected.

In the spring a hard core of mediocrity remained from the year before. Most of the good looking youngsters proved to be still some time away. Since the club had only been in existence two years the management didn't have the over-all personnel with which to make wholesale trades.

The one big one they had been able to fashion during the off-season did not work out as well as expected. They gave Roger Craig, the classic loser, to the Cardinals for Outfielder George Altman and Bill Wakefield, a young pitcher. They hoped Altman would go back to his form of 1962, when he hit 22 home runs and .321 for the Chicago Cubs. He had dipped to .274 with the Cards in 1963. Plagued by injuries almost from the season's start, he was in and out of the Met lineup and hit only .230.

Their best additions to the cast came later. In June they obtained Roy McMillan, a 34-year-old shortstop with twelve-year service stripes in the National League, for Jay Hook and a fat bundle of cash. For the first time the Mets owned a shortstop who wasn't at the mercy of a ground ball.

Pitchers who used to shut their eyes and say a silent prayer when a ball went that way, were soon pop-eyed at his wide range and knowledge. The quiet veteran's influence was felt as much in the clubhouse as on the field. Hot-foots and other childish horseplay before and after games went out of style.

Much earlier in the season they had purchased Charley Smith, a 26-year-old third baseman from the Chicago White Sox. Later, because he was judged allergic to bunts, among other things, Smith was tried in left field. His over-all batting average was only .239 for the season but he led the club in homers with 20.

In June they bought Frank Lary from Detroit in time to get some highly professional jobs of pitching from the veteran before passing him on to Milwaukee for Dennis Ribant, a young righthander who soon proved worthy of a starter's status.

When injuries hit the Mets the result was sometimes catastrophic because there were seldom adequate replacements on the bench. They had many hurts and it figured that the first would happen in Mexico City—only a Met could get hurt on foreign soil. This was on March 7, when Jim Hickman jammed an ankle stepping on a base as loose as a jumping bean. Cleón Jones, a promising outfielder, and Ed Kranepool, suffered bad reactions to typhoid shots for the Mexican trip. Jones wound up back in Buffalo. So did Kranepool when he reported overweight, then pulled a leg muscle.

Carl Willey, a nine-game winner the season before and potentially the ace of the staff when the new one started, was the best pitcher in Florida by April 3. He had gone

26 innings without a run. Then, in an exhibition game with Detroit, the quiet man from Maine had his jaw broken by a drive off the bat of Gates Brown, a Tiger rookie. He was sidelined for two months, then tried to pitch too soon and developed arm trouble. He appeared in only 14 games, two as the starting pitcher, before being sent home.

(There must have been Mets fans at Yankee Stadium one midsummer afternoon when Detroit was the visiting club. When Gates Brown, a total stranger, was introduced as a pinch-hitter, Met banners were waved and Brown lustily booed.)

Larry Bearnarth, so effective as a relief jobber the season before, began to suffer from shoulder trouble not many weeks after the start. Tracey Stallard also came down with occasional arm miseries; Ron Hunt had to fight injuries like a hockey player most of the season and there were many others.

Sometimes the hurts came in waves. On June 29 in San Francisco, Gus Mauch, the trainer, had to send five men to the hospital for x-rays. They were Ron Hunt and his bad right toe, Chris Cannizzaro and his damaged left thumb; John Stephenson and a bad left shin; Bill Hunter and a liner-banged left knee-cap and Tim Harkness and his ailing right knee.

"When your pitcher goes out to start against us today we may not be there," Casey Stengel told Al Dark, the manager of the Giants before the game. "Most of my men are in the hospital posin' for a team x-ray picture. It may be featured in the club's year book later."

Chez Stengel, otherwise Shea Stadium, was a fun-house, almost always crowded, and the club cashier laughed all the way to the bank. But putting one little win after another was hard. Five victories were the most they could ever put together. There were, on the other hand, two eight-game losing streaks and one month (June) in which only eight games were won.

It was catch-as-catch-can behind the plate most of the way. Jesse Gonder had the edge at first because his bat had a reputation, but later Hawk Taylor and Chris Cannizzaro got more duty there. Sometimes Stengel, the democratic manager, would ask the starting pitcher to name the man. This frequently turned out to be Cannizzaro, the owner of a fine arm. When he also began to hit with authority Cannizzaro had the Number One job more or less locked up. Then he too was injured.

The infield and outfield were unsettled as South American politics. Duke Snider, apparently less happy than the year before, was sold to the Giants early. Frank Thomas was in and out of the lineup with assorted disturbances until he was shipped to the Phillies late in the season. George Altman, Smith and others were used in left field. Jim Hickman labored more than anyone else in the center-field, though sometimes Rod Kanehl, the super sub, and Larry Elliott bobbed up there.

The solid one proved to be Joe Christopher, who hit .300 and led in runs-batted-in with 76 in 154 games. The season before he had played in only 119 and hit .244.

An impressively constructed man with speed, he some-times set a careening course when he went after a fly ball.

"But if I can play regularly for a month," Christopher said early in the year, "I'll show them a big league hitter. I can hit, I can run and I can throw but nobody ever gave me a chance."

He got his chance this time when Altman, tabbed the regular rightfielder, was injured early. Stengel stayed with him and Christopher, in his 10th year in professional baseball, bloomed as a consistent hitter who frequently delivered the long ball.

The shortstop problem was solved by McMillan's

arrival, and Ed Kranepool, his first base (and other) lessons learned after three weeks with Buffalo, came back to take over the first base job, this time for keeps.

Ron Hunt, who led the club in hitting with .303, was such a respected performer the players of the league voted him the National's second baseman for the All Star game, the first Met to win a starting role. Later, between injuries, he played third base as well as second. Bobby Klauss, a fine double-play operative at second, was obtained late in the season from Cincinnati for Tim Harkness.

Sometimes the pitching wasn't too bad. It was worse. It was thin almost from the start because of the injury to Willey and Bearnarth's trouble. If a Met delivered virtuoso pitching one time, he was bound to get bombed out of sight the next time he showed up.

Al Jackson, the little workhorse among the starters, had his fine games and stretches in which he just couldn't win. He again led the club in shutouts (three) and won the most games (eleven). Jack Fisher, who had been used only in batting practice for a while by the Giants the previous summer, came on to win ten games. Tracey Stallard also took ten, some of them spectacular jobs. Galen Cisco won only six but was the club's most effective pitcher late in the season until he too was injured. Bill Wakefield, regarded as a throw-in in the Altman deal with St. Louis, contributed a number of fine relief jobs and appeared in the most games (62).

When the New York Sales Executives Club named Casey Stengel Salesman of the Year they had in mind, of course, the job he did putting the Mets across to the public. Just as important was the job of selling he did to the many infant Mets.

In spring training it sometimes seemed like the Children's Hour as the Professor held forth at the ball yard or in the lobby of the St. Petersburg Beach motel to such embryo Mets as Jerry Hinsley, an 18-year-old pitcher with no professional experience; Ron Swoboda, a muscular 19-year-old outfielder plucked from the University of Maryland campus; Ron Locke, a 22-year-old lefthander; Bill Wakefield, 23, righthanded and the owner of a hard fastball and a bachelor's degree in economics from Stanford University; John Stephenson, a 23-year-old catcher, and Dick Gardner, a lefthander who had struck out 220 men in 35 games in the Florida State League.

"My high school teacher back in Binghampton warned me that I might wind up in Mexico some day," said Gardner on the eve of the club's trip to Mexico City for exhibition games. "I thought it was a lot of bull. Now I'm sorry I wound up with bad marks."

Among other distinctions Hinsley became the Mets' first player-reporter. "By Jerry Hinsley," the diary of a Met rookie, began appearing in the New York *Journal-American* in the spring and continued until he was farmed out for more seasoning.

"Cheap hits almost killed me in the game with the Cubs last night," began his story the day after he started against Chicago in late April.

"Hey, you'd better let me see my story after you write it," he said to Barney Kremenko, his ghost-writer.

Later, in St. Louis, Hinsley and Stephenson were returning to their room when Professor Stengel caught up with them at the elevator. He told them to tag along to his room so he could ask them two or three questions.

"We were going to go over to the zoo in Forest Park," said Stephenson. "But this was just as entertaining. I could listen to him all day and I did."

"It did me good, what I remember of it," said Hinsley.

Herman Lautenschlager, of the Shagwong Inn, Montauk Point, had the honor of being labeled the one millionth fan of the first season at Shea until the rains came one night and wiped the game away before it had run long enough to be official.

"I feel like Roger Craig used to," said the almost-one-millionth fan after the announcement that the game had been postponed. "Feel like here I am winning a big one and then—boom—the sky falls in."

Mr. Lautenschlager wasn't the only guest of some distinction. One night Bill McEvoy, 23, a mailman and baseball lover, was watching the Mets lose a 6–2 game to the Phillies. He got fed up and decided to show the Mets a thing or two. Putting aside his container of beer he left his buddies in the upper deck, went downstairs, hopped a railing and galloped onto the basepaths. He slid into second base as Ron Hunt stood there stunned. "This man was just trying to show the Mets something about the game. He was so disappointed at their poor showing," Harry Harrison, his attorney, told a judge later.

Said Judge Bernard Dubin in Queens Court: "This is a very unusual case. The Mets can certainly do a lot of things to a lot of people.

"Don't you think the Mets have enough trouble without you?" he asked McEvoy. "You unnerved the players. These are professional ball players [that's what the judge said] and the fans are paying to see them play, not you."

McEvoy had tried to strike up a conversation with Hunt, but Ron told him, "Look, buddy, you better get out of here fast—here come the house cops. You may be faster than they are but there are more of 'em."

Other things not on the National League schedule happened at Shea.

On an off day the Mets, their wives, Casey and Edna Stengel, the TV and radio men and the journalists were guests at a monster clambake thrown by the Bangor *Daily News* in honor of Carl Willey. Sports Editor Owen

Osborne brought Red McMann, a round gentleman from Bath, Maine, who cooks up clambakes for people, down to Shea along with a staff of ten assistants. Because of wet weather McMann and his men cooked the clams, lobsters and sweet corn in left field at the club level and cracked the concrete. They cooked five bushels of clams and 250 lobsters, then served wild blueberry pie for dessert.

The Yankees went to Shea to play the second annual game for the Mayor's Trophy, as well as the Department of Sanitation's Golden Can, on June 15, but it rained the game away. When they finally played it on August 24, the Yankees won it, 6–4.

The banners were out in force. "Ban the Bronx Bombers," read one, "Hello Yogi and His Harmonicats," said another.

With the Yankees ahead, 4–3, in the seventh inning, two of them got on base and there was a chance to get some insurance runs. Berra looked up and down his bench but there was no pinch-hitter in sight. He grabbed a bat and went up himself. He grounded into a double-play but the noise of Yogi's welcome by the fans was still echoing when he went back to the dugout.

THAT WAS THE YEAR THAT WAS

It was agreed that when they got around to building the Mets' own Hall of Fame there would be something, somewhere in that magnificent museum that would tell of their most memorable games. It wouldn't do to just have the caps and bells of the jesters, the gloves of the foremost fumblers, the bronzed shoes of the leading wrong-way runners and the bats and portraits of the heroes enshrined. There would also have to be some blow by blow accounts of how they did and didn't do it.

There would be accounts of the victories their followers liked to recall after each season, not only because there were so few of them but because they so often had a special flavor, like fairy tales or stories of the poor but honest citizens who every once in a while hit Bingo.

There would be unforgettable defeats too. The Mets specialized in them and many stayed with a man, like a king-sized hangover, so that days later he would still be bragging that no team in the long history of baseball could lose with the artistry of the Mets.

Researchers submitted that these were the most memorable games of the 1964 season:

It began woefully. Their first game of the new season resulted in an ordinary 5–3, run-of-the-mill defeat in Philadelphia, but that very next afternoon the Mets demonstrated that they had retained their old ability to lose the hard way—to come up with the big error and the wrong pitch at the crucial moment—when they lost again to the Phillies. Their first baseman dropped a thrown ball with two out in the eighth inning, and the next one pitched was clobbered for a home run.

Tracey Stallard was dueling Jim Bunning, the refugee Detroit Tiger and one-time strikeout emperor of the American League, with somewhat surprising skill. A careful Casey Stengel had put Jack Fisher on a standby basis in the bullpen in case Stallard faltered, but he didn't. His boy held the Phils to five hits, didn't walk a man and was tied with Bunning 1–1 at the end of seven innings.

Bobby Wine started the Philadelphia eighth with a double down the left field line, but Stallard took good care of the next two batters. Richie Allen then grounded to second and for all intents and purposes the inning was over as Amado Samuel fetched the ball and made a routine throw to first base. Tim Harkness dropped the ball, however, all hands were safe and the Phils had another shot. Tony Gonzales, the next hitter, lined into the left field stands for a 4–1 lead. It meant the ball game when Bunning shut the door on the Mets in the ninth, striking out the side.

WOE, WOE, AND THEN SOME

Everything was in order for a gala getaway in gleaming new Shea Stadium when the Mets returned from the first two games in Philadelphia to start the home season on Friday, April 17. The field, a soggy green carpet not long before, had been rolled almost dry; the escalators ran perfectly; the freshly frocked ushers and the pretty usherettes, the latter dressed in natty orange and blue uniforms with similarly-striped bands on their straw hats, smiled welcomes. A happy crowd of 50,132 customers poured into the five multi-colored seating levels. Planes from nearby LaGuardia Field, roaring low overhead, added to the din of Guy Lombardo's band music and the bugle-blowing, drum-beating, bell-ringing fans.

Everything was in order but the Mets. The first pitch by their man Jack Fisher was a strike and the first rally was by the home team, but that about ended their notable achievements. The Pittsburgh Pirates, attending strictly to business, recovered from a three-run outburst by the Mets in the fourth inning, caught them in the seventh and passed them in the ninth. The Pirates got 16 of the day's 23 hits; the first one was a home run inside the left field foul-line by Willie Stargell, the Pittsburgh leftfielder, in the second inning.

There was excitement in the fourth when Ron Hunt doubled and Jesse Gonder hit a scoring single into right field for the first New York run off Bob Friend in 51 innings pitched against them over a three-year period. And more of the same when Frank Thomas singled, Jim Hickman was hit by a pitch and Amado Samuel doubled down the left field line to score both and put the Mets ahead 3–1.

They could stay on top, however, for only three innings. With two out in the fifth, Roberto Clemente singled and Stargell doubled him home. In the seventh Clemente and Stargell chased Fisher with successive singles. Jack Banta was the relief pitcher as Donn Clendenon dribbled one past the shortstop to score Clemente with the run that put Pittsburgh ahead. In the ninth Stargell singled for his fourth hit, took second on another single by Clendenon and scored on one by Bill Mazerowski. In the end the big, handsome $1,500,000 scoreboard sadly read: "Pittsburgh 4, Mets 3."

Stargell, the visitor who distinguished himself, was asked afterward how he liked Shea Stadium.

"Beautiful," answered the young man, "just beautiful. When you're in the outfield those yellow seats sometimes make it hard to find the ball hit against that background, but the visibility is the best in the league. The hitting— that's no problem at all."

On May 15, the Mets winged 3,000 miles across the continent, landed in San Francisco, did a dozen or so pushups and went on to beat the Giants, 4–2. It was their third straight win and the sixth in nine games. Charlie Smith's two-run double in the eighth was the big blow, but just as important was the fact that Tracey Stallard held Willie Mays hitless.

The next afternoon they were one out away from yet another decision over the Giants but the man they had to get out was Mays again. This time Willie drove the first pitch over the right field fence for his 14th home run of the season. It tied the score 4–4 and Jim Davenport untied it for the Giants with a two-out, two-run homer in the 15th.

Never on Sunday had the Mets managed to win a road game this season until they upended the Cardinals, 3–2, in the first game of a double-header on July 19. It looked like a double delight when Frank Lary, who hadn't allowed a run since the second inning and only four hits from the third through the eighth, rolled into the ninth of the second game holding a 6–3 lead.

Then the Cards, with an assist from the unbearable heat (the Sportsmans Park concession people could have saved gas that afternoon by broiling the hot dogs and hamburgers in the sun) got to the veteran. Carl Warwick, a pinch-hitter, cracked a double and Curt Flood singled him to third. Stengel removed the wilting Lary in favor of Bill Hunter, but Lou Brock singled and then Ken Boyer doubled to tie the score. Darrell Sutherland relieved Hunter but the ball Dick Groat then slapped on the ground took a hop high over Ron Hunt's head and White scored to give the Cards the game, 7–6.

Larry Bearnarth, for one, won't forget the night of April 29 in St. Louis in a hurry. The game stood 3–2 in favor of the Mets until the seventh inning when the Cardinals tied it up. Bill Wakefield went out for a pinch-hitter in the tenth and Bearnarth became the Mets' third relief jobber. He got out of trouble when Bill White, after moving Carl Warwick to third with a liner off the right field wall, was caught at second base by an alert relay for the third out.

He was soon beyond help, however, in the eleventh. Ken Boyer initiated the sad story with a single through the pitcher's box. The next batter, Tim McCarver, wanted to move his man along with a bunt but Bearnarth wouldn't let him. Larry had been burned when he let Manny Motta bunt a fat pitch in the ninth inning of a game in Pittsburgh a few days before and the game was lost.

Bearnarth brushed McCarver back with an inside pitch. He knocked the Cards' catcher down with another. He eventually lost the plate and McCarver took first base on a fourth ball. Mike Shannon sacrificed both runners further along with a bunt, so with first base open, Julian Javier was intentionally walked. When Bearnarth couldn't come in with a 3–1 pitch to pinch-hitter Joeff Long with the bases loaded, the unintentional base on balls to that citizen confirmed the inevitable 4–3 St. Louis victory.

Had Marvelous Marv' Thorneberry still been among those present he undoubtedly would have observed afterwards, "It's just hard to believe one team can be so unlucky."

Sometimes Shea Stadium settled for a hero other than one of the Mets. Such a day was Sunday, June 21, when 32,904 witnessed Jim Bunning pitch a perfect game as he beat the Mets for the Phillies, 6–0.

It became a pleasure as they realized what Bunning, the 38-year-old who was traded away by the Detroit Tigers the previous winter, was threatening to accomplish despite the Mets and the 91-degree heat. Only one ball came close to being a hit. In the fifth Jesse Gonder drove a liner toward right field. Second baseman Tony Taylor ran hard to his left, dove and knocked the ball down. Then he threw Gonder out by several feet.

By the seventh inning, when Bunning was seven outs away from Cooperstown canonization, the customers were loudly rooting him on. The Mets had become the villains and the visiting pitcher the hero. When Bunning batted in the ninth he was wildly cheered. The fans were still shouting when Charlie Smith fouled out to start the Mets' half of the last inning. They booed when George Altman was announced as a pinch-hitter, cheered when he struck out. Rookie John Stephenson next carried his .047 batting average to the plate. When Bunning fanned him for the 27th and last out he received a standing ovation that lasted many minutes.

The Phils scored once in the first and once in the second. In the sixth they knocked out Tracey Stallard and scored four more times, permitting their man to work on perfection without worrying overmuch about winning.

The considerable fuss over Bunning's fancy feat was easy to understand. The previous perfect game in the National League was in 1880. The last one pitched in the majors was in the fifth game of the 1958 World Series, when Don Larsen of the Yankees didn't let one of the Brooklyn Dodgers reach first base as he won at Yankee Stadium, 2–0.

Mary Bunning and her daughter Barbara had expected to visit the World's Fair across the way with Jim after the Phils were through with the Mets. They never got there and, of course, they didn't care. They were called onto the field to buss Jim and take television bows with him on Ralph Kiner's after-the-game show. Then they stayed around while the Phillies won the second game 8–2. They had to stay because by now Jim Bunning was getting all manner of offers through Frank Scott, the player's agent. When he was offered something like $3,000 to appear on the Ed Sullivan Show that night, the World's Fair visit was postponed until the club's next visit to Shea Stadium.

The Mets were more or less used to being beaten by the bats swung by such celebrated citizens as Willie Mays, Jim Davenport, Frank Howard, Tommy Davis, Hank Aaron, Eddie Mathews, Ernie Banks, Dick Groat, Roberto Clemente and the like. Those were all established swingers, many of them owning fat past performance papers against New York pitching. But it really hurt way down deep when they were beaten, 4–3, in the tenth inning of a game in Chicago on August 30 by a Cub who took a .050 batting average into the game.

Because he had made only one hit in 20 times at bat in April, Ellis Burton, a much-traveled 28-year-old outfielder, had been deemed expendable and farmed out to the Fort Worth Texas League club. Now, with Outfielder Doug Clemens injured, they called him back. He had barely time to unpack before being put into the lineup against the Mets.

Burton struck out his first time up. He singled in the fourth but it was, after all, only his third hit of the season. In the 10th, however, he came up after Jim Steward had doubled and hit a scoring single to beat Galen Cisco and ruin the Mets' bid for their 13th August victory, the most in one month during the three years of their existence.

Baseball's longest day began at Shea Stadium at 1:05 on the sunny afternoon of Sunday, May 31, and ended at 11:25 o'clock that night—10 hours and 20 minutes later. When it was all over the Mets had lost two games to the San Francisco Giants, 5–3 and 8–2, the second in 23 innings; 57,037 customers had consumed 21,236 cans of beer, 28,915 containers of soda pop, 12,566 hot dogs, 6,502 bags of peanuts and countless other concession goodies. Umpires Ed Suder, Paul Proyer, Ed Secory, and Ken Burkhart, for whom a between-the-games meal was somehow forgotten in the confusion, sat down to belated steaks, and the worn bodies of the Giants were shipped back to their New York hotel by bus.

And the Mets? They scrambled wearily to home or restaurant for food. Their only nourishment between games had been some chicken broth. Then to bed.

Although the next day was an idle one in the schedule, an exhibition game had been carded for that Monday night with their Eastern League farm club in Williamsport, Pa. Only 11 men on the squad were excused and Road Secretary Lou Niss went around the clubhouse reminding the famished, weary players who were to go when to catch the bus for the airport. It rained in Williamsport the next day but even before word of this blessing had been received Casey Stengel had made the proper appeal for a postponement. The Mets were called early and told to go back to bed.

The second game, the 23-inning marathon, consumed a total of 7 hours and 23 minutes, the longest game in baseball history on a time basis.

The end came when Amado Samuel of the Mets made the final out. A little while before, the Giants had broken a 15-inning scoreless stretch with two runs in the 23rd with two out. Jim Davenport started it with a triple to the right field corner. Cap Peterson was intentionally walked and Del Crandell, a pinch-hitter, drove in the first run with a right field ground rule double. Then Jay Alou batted in the insurance run with another single.

Galen Cisco, who had gone to the bullpen in case he was needed to pitch an inning or two, was the sixth New York pitcher and the loser after nine innings of fine, five-hit relief pitching. He had pitched seven innings two days before. The winner was Gaylord Perry, who worked ten innings and allowed only seven hits.

Ed Kranepool, the Mets' teen-age first baseman, had

been recalled from the Buffalo farm club after playing a double-header Saturday in Syracuse, where he collected four singles, a double and two home runs in 10 trips to the plate.

He caught a plane out of Buffalo early Sunday morning, took a bus to New York, then a taxi to Shea Stadium and arrived at 10:30 A.M. Then he played the day's 32 innings of baseball on six hours' sleep and one bowl of soup.

"He must have been a pretty tired boy," said his mother, "because I was tired just watching him." Mrs. Kranepool stayed at Shea until both games were over because she had her son's car keys and house keys.

JOY

The Pittsburgh Pirates made life miserable for the Mets on Opening Day in Shea Stadium, leading the more caustic critics to predict that it would be another one of those Aprils—full of showers, flowers and Met losses. To start the 1962 season, they had dropped nine in a row; they lost their first eight games in 1963; and now they had started life in their new playpen with four successive defeats.

Al Jackson came through with a six-hit shutout of the Pirates on Sunday, April 19, however, the 10–6 win ending their perennial starting streak at four. His helpers were on their best batting behavior too, knocking Bob Veale out of sight in the fourth inning when they batted across four of their six runs.

Jackson, no stranger to late-inning tragedy, survived threats by the Pirates late in the game. He struck out Willie Stargell for the third time to start the ninth inning, got Donn Clendenon to pop-up, Bob Bailey on an easy fly, and walked off to the tumultuous appreciation of 30,185 fans.

The Mets made Sunday, May 10, Beat-an-Old-Buddy-Day at Shea Stadium when they met Roger Craig for the first time since he had moved to the St. Louis Cardinals. They defeated him, 4–1.

It took a lot of doing, for Craig proved as hard to pry runs out of as he had on many an afternoon while toiling for the Mets. The Mets loaded the bases on Craig with none out in the first inning but they couldn't score. They succeeded, finally, in the sixth when Roy McMillan, who had opened the first with a double, tripled and scored on George Altman's single. Then the Cards got a run from Tracey Stallard in the seventh to tie things up.

Rod Kanehl startled Craig and practically everyone else in the place, including himself, with a home run with one out in the eighth. Ron Hunt, his roomie, nearly duplicated Rod's shot but the ball hit close to the top of the left field fence and bounded back onto the field for a double. Hunt scored and Craig got the hook when Jim Hickman singled. Lew Burdette came in and hardly had time to moisten the ball before Frank Thomas drove it over the fence.

Kanehl, 254 times at bat when they closed the books October 4, didn't hit another home run all season.

JOY UNCONFINED

A home run, this time by a Met who was rusty from illness-enforced idleness, beat the Cardinals again on July 9.

Al Jackson, trying to free himself from a seven-game losing streak, had pitched well against the Cards' Curt Simmons. He gave up two runs in the first inning, helped get them back with a single that triggered a two-run rally in the third and fell behind again in the seventh. He had held the Cards to seven hits in making his first start since June 18, but with the Cards leading 3–2 in the ninth, it seemed as though the little lefty's fine effort would be wasted.

Joe Christopher poked one of Simmons' changeups into left field for a single, but Simmons seemed safe enough when George Altman and Jim Hickman were retired. Roy McMillan, back at shortstop for the first time in three weeks, was the next batter listed, but Casey Stengel asked bench-sitter Frank Thomas if he felt strong enough to pinch-hit. Thomas, twice hospitalized by a glandular infection, had returned to uniform but a few days before.

"Well, I can swing," he told Casey, and grabbed his bat.

Thomas swung and Simmons' pitch disappeared over the left field fence, beating the Cardinals, 4–3.

"You," yelled Jackson as he went out to greet Thomas at home plate, "You are one helluva fine morale builder!"

You think Chicago was shocked by the St. Valentine Day's Massacre? Do you suppose that toddlin' town was startled by Little Egypt's first gyrations? These were ho-hum events compared to what happened at Wrigley Field on the afternoon of May 26.

The lowly Mets had just escaped from a horrible week end in Houston, where they had taken a Saturday night bath, 8–4, 4–0, and then, after a four-hour-and-42-minute double-header defeat (the second game began at 11 P.M.), had been slapped with a Sunday shutout by the same Colts, 5–0.

They arrived in Chicago with their bats and bodies dragging, their spirits lower than a deep sea diver with a bad case of the bends. George Altman and Tim Harkness, regarded at the moment as regulars, couldn't play because of injuries, and the rest of them were worn and weary.

Professor Stengel, though he noticed the stiff wind blowing toward right field favoring lefthanded hitters, and knew that Bob Buhl, a righthander, was Chicago's starting pitcher, packed his lineup with righthanded hitters. The resulting earthquake, noted on sensitive Chicago seismographs, read: Mets 19, Cubs 1.

The Mets, who went into the game suffering from a streak of 19 straight scoreless innings, scored four runs in the first, three in the second, a measly two in the fifth, four in the seventh and then a fat six, just to be even more emphatic about it, in the ninth.

They set all manner of club batting records against six

stunned Chicago pitchers. When the dust at Wrigley Field had settled it was discovered that they had set marks for most runs (19), most hits (23), most runs-batted-in (17) and most hits in one game by·a player (Dick Smith with five).

Stengel had said before the game that he planned to play his "most rested" platoon. Smith was a perfect example. He had seen only fill-in duty in Houston, hadn't played in Sunday's game at all. On this titanic Tuesday he was the Mets' lead-off batter, and started with a bunt single in the first. Then he hit two solid singles, then a double and finally a triple in the ninth. He was obviously just getting warmed up when the game ended.

It was a memorable game too for Jack Fisher, not only because he was the beneficiary of all this hitting, but also because he pitched a complete game for the first time as a Met. He held the Cubs to four hits and would have had a shutout but for Billy Cowan's single with two out in the fifth. The hit scored Ernie Banks, who had led off with a double.

"I'm not gonna' leave the hotel tonight," announced Stengel afterwards. "Because I'll probably be gettin' a phone call from Mr. Wrigley of the Cubs askin' if he can't please have some of our treeeemendous hitters in a trade."

The Mets were losing to the Cardinals at Shea Stadium, 1–0, in the seventh inning. They were losing it, moreover, to old buddy Roger Craig. The size of the crowd reflected the lateness of the season. It was September 24, 11 days before the end and only 3,941 customers, their smallest audience of the year, sat in the stands.

Billy Klauss opened the seventh with a double and Ed Kranepool scored him with another to tie the score. Ron Hunt, who had been playing for almost three weeks with a bad back, a sore heel and a chronic sore toe, was up

there to move Kranepool to third with a sacrifice bunt.
He dropped the ball down and Craig came off the mound
to fetch it, then threw to Julian Javier, covering first base
in the bunt situation. There was a cloud of dust as Hunt
slid head-first into the bag. Then another in right field,
where Craig's errant throw had gone. Kranepool crossed
the plate standing up. The 2–1 victory was the Met's 51st,
a will-o'-the-wisp they had been chasing unsuccessfully
for their last four games, losing all four by one run. It
equalled their win total of the previous season and left
them time to achieve a record-breaking 52, or more!

Sometimes the Mets won, if you believed the historians
who chronicled the capers of the club, because Casey
Stengel put a curse of sorts on the opposition. Only Casey
called it his "Whommy."

"I use it almost every time we play the Reds," he said
after a 4–3 10-inning win in Cincinnati on July 22. "It
worked in the double-header we took from them a week
ago Sunday an' it's worked the last two nights here.

"I don't," he added with a chuckle, "use it against
Los Angeles."

The Mets had at that point lost nine out of 10 games
to the Dodgers, whereas they had taken six out of 10 from
the Reds.

The Reds, desperate, turned to a running game that
night. They made 15 hits but could score only three runs,
as three men were thrown out at home plate and another
was cut down trying to gain third.

"They thought maybe they could wear out home plate,"
explained Casey. "But the whommy kept it away from
them. The plate was movin'."

Once again Ron Hunt's hard-nose head-first slide into
first base made the difference. The score was tied 1–1
when he started the tenth inning with an infield single,

getting the safe call from Umpire Stan Landes. He went into first like a man into a swimming pool.

George Altman struck out, but Willard Hunter, the relief pitcher, was able to bunt Hunt to second. Then Jim Hickman, batting for Larry Elliott, belted the ball past third base to score Hunt.

Hunt hit Frank Robinson with a pitch at the start of the Cincinnati tenth. With two out, Robinson stole second. Leo Cardenas was the next Redleg batter and he hit a line drive to centerfield that seemed a sure base hit. In the Met dugout Stengel leaped to his feet and waved his arms feverishly at the ball, muttering all the while. Hickman, in centerfield now, got a bad jump on the drive but it stayed up there long enough for him to catch up to it for the third out. The whommy had worked again.

He wasn't complaining, mind you, but too many times Tracey Stallard turned up as the fall guy for some other fellow's heroic feat.

There was the day in Boston in 1961, when Tracey, toiling for the Red Sox, served up the pitch that Roger Maris belted for his 61st home run, busting George Herman (Babe) Ruth's long-revered record. Forgotten was the fact that he lost a tough 1–0 ball game in the process.

The years went by and he became a Met, but it seemed as though he still had to keep a rendezvous with somebody else seeking the jackpot. On June 21 at Shea Stadium Philadelphia's Jim Bunning pitched his perfect no-hit-no-run game against the Mets. Stallard, naturally, was the losing pitcher.

He seemed like the understander in an acrobatic act, the man at the bottom of the pile. He labored long and he labored hard but it often was in vain. On five occasions this season he had been the pitcher in a game in which the other fellow shut the Mets out.

On September 16 in San Francisco, Stallard at long last had an altogether enjoyable afternoon. With the Giants still in the race he stopped them with a 4–0 shutout. He also tied two medium-sized Met records, striking out ten men, to tie a club record shared by Jay Hook and Dennis Ribant. And he scored his tenth win, tying Roger Craig and Jack Fisher for the achievement by a Met righthander.

This time he received formidable support from his companions, notably George Altman who belabored Gaylord Perry, who in turn had won five straight games from the Mets and allowed them only two runs in 42 innings, for a homer, a double and a single.

The Milwaukee Braves, running nine games behind the league-leading Phillies, thought they might still have a shot at the National League pennant if they could get some experienced pitching help. On August 8 they decided that they would rather have 33-year-old Frank Lary, owner of a two-win, three-loss record with the Mets, than a kid pitcher with a nine-win, two-loss record on their Denver farm club. They agreed to hand Dennis Ribant, a 22-year-old bonus baby righthander, to the Mets in exchange for Lary and some fresh cabbage from the Mets' mint.

As a former junior hockey player in the Detroit Red Wing organization, Ribant was used to being thrown into action in a hurry. Thus he wasn't a bit disturbed when Casey Stengel started him in Pittsburgh, three days after he reported. He was more disturbed, probably, by the three-run homer outfielder Jerry Lynch of the Pirates hit off him in the fifth inning of the game, which was lost, eventually, 5–4. What disturbed him most, perhaps, was the announcement over the public address system that

Lynch's drive to the 70-foot high roof of Forbes Field, at a point 325 feet along the ground, was only the sixth hit into that neighborhood since 1925.

Five days later Casey threw him against the Pirates again, this time at Shea Stadium. He came back with a four-hit, 5–0 shutout for his first major league victory. Charlie Smith helped him with a three-run homer in the first inning and another, his fifteenth of the season, in the eighth.

In the meantime the youngster helped himself. Bill Mazeroski and Jim Pagliaroni hit back-to-back singles with one out in the fifth. When Smith bobbled the ball Mazeroski moved to third, the only Pirate to advance beyond first base. Ribant got out of trouble by striking out Dick Schofield and grabbing a wicked hopper by Bob Veale for a putout at first base.

He admitted afterwards that he had the shakes at times, mostly because of Lynch and the tape-measure homer the outfielder had hit in Pittsburgh.

"I didn't want any more of those," he said. "I talked to Mel Harder (the Mets' pitching coach) the first two times Lynch and (Willie) Stargell came up."

In the ninth Ribant closed out the affair in style. He got Bill Virdon on a grounder to first base, threw out Roberto Clemente, the league's leading hitter himself, and then struck out Lynch.

NOW WHAT?

In September of '64, Bing Devine, who had been fired as master tradesman of the St. Louis Cardinals in August, was signed as special assistant to Met President George Weiss. Eddie Stanky, who quit the St. Louis organization hours after Devine was tagged out, also joined the Mets. He was named the club's trouble-shooter, the same job he had held with the Cardinals.

Shortly afterwards the Mets' Senior Citizens clan grew with the addition of Warren Spahn. Casey Stengel, the dean, was 74 on July 31, 1964. Berra was 39 when he moved over from the Yankees. Spahn, a Brave of either the Boston or Milwaukee variety since he first came up to pitch from the Hartford club of the Eastern League in 1942, became a 43-year-old Met.

"Only Stengel," observed Francis Stann, in the Washington *Star*, "is definitely not scheduled to play in 1965."

Spahn, the hawk-nosed lefthander who had 13 20-win seasons, a record, had only a 6-13 mark with Milwaukee in 1964. He thought out loud that his lack of success with the Braves was due to lack of regular work. He was added to the roster as a pitcher-coach via a cash deal believed to have amounted to $20,000.

The Mets took over a contract under which Spahn received a reported $80,000 salary. They added that he was not asked to take the maximum 25 per cent cut. In any event they would be paying him more than anybody on the club save Stengel.

"I'll be a pitcher first and a coach after that," he promised. "I think the two jobs can be separate. I always did some coaching even when I didn't have that title. I always worked with the Braves' young pitchers in spring training camp and enjoyed it.

"Physically I'm sound and I refuse to believe that I could slide downhill as fast as Milwaukee said I did last season. Every year I'm a slow starter and last spring I had more trouble than usual getting sharp. Later on I didn't get the chances to pitch when I was ready. I've got 356 wins in the book now and I'd like to make it 400."

The memory of Yogi Berra's reception at the Mayor's Trophy Game in June had stayed with George Weiss. Casey Stengel had signed to manage all over again in late September, scotching reports that he would become general manager of the Los Angeles Angels, or run for President. Then Yogi, whom Casey, with a grin, often called his assistant manager when he was Yankee boss, had the rug pulled from under him. Although the Yankees won the pennant in his first run as a manager, they told him the job was no longer his, and offered him a spot scouting and serving as a general trouble-shooter for Ralph Houk in the farm system.

The Mets hurried to offer him a job as one of Stengel's assistants. Yogi took the offer to Pinehurst, North Carolina, with him when he went on a golfing trip with friends. Without question, separation from the Yankee organization, which he served for 22 years, was a wrench.

Berra believed that he still belonged in uniform. He had to think of his side job as a vice president of the Yoo Hoo Beverage Company. His name would be worth a lot more to the chocolate drink firm if he was still visible in a baseball suit instead of sitting in the stands as a Yankee scout, or inhabiting the club's office. On November 17, he signed a two-year contract at $40,000 with the Mets, to coach, maybe catch a bit if his body responded in spring training, and to be possible successor to Stengel.

Driving to Shea from New Jersey through the heavy traffic, people recognized Yogi and kept yelling congratulations.

"Going to the Mets, hey Yogi?" they kept shouting. "Great, great!"

"I'm not sore," Yogi said. "The Yanks were good to me. The Cardinals and Browns didn't want me in St. Louis, my home town. But the Yankees signed me, sight unseen. It's good to be back with Casey, though. Real good."

Warren Spahn, talking to his first New York audience, said, "I hear Yogi will be reactivated as a player if he has a good spring training. I'm looking forward to pitching to him, particularly if Yogi is still talking to the hitters the way he did to us in those World Series games. He talked so much you'd forget the ball and strike count."

"Do you suppose you and Yogi would be the oldest battery ever to appear in the major leagues?" someone asked.

"What difference would that make?" Spahn countered with a shrug. "We'd probably be the ugliest by far."

"I resent that," grunted Yogi, who was sitting close by.

"Anyway," continued Spahn, "I think that fellows like Yogi and myself have something to offer a young club like the Mets. We both played on winning ball clubs and we know what winning baseball is all about. We can help the kids."

In December the Mets traded pitcher Tracey Stallard to the Cardinals in return for two highly-regarded youngsters—Outfielder Johnny Lewis and lefthanded pitcher Gordon Richardson. This was at the urging of Devine, who had brought Lou Brock, Bill White, Dick Groat, Curt Flood and others to St. Louis after succeeding Frank Lane as general manager of that club in 1957.

"Lewis could become our centerfielder," said Devine after the deal. "He may have some trouble hitting the lefthanders for a while but that doesn't mean he won't make it. There's nothing wrong with the idea of platooning a youngster until he gets both his feet on the ground. And Casey Stengel's always been great at that. He plays a boy a week or so, then hides him a while, then plays him again."

Devine added that he and Weiss were working on a five-year plan for the Mets.

"We had such a plan in St. Louis," he said. "After five years we were still struggling, then last season everything fell into place and the club won. It took time but St. Louis finally had a championship club.

"We won't expect miracles but I'm sure that by 1965 the Mets will be right up there with the pennant contenders.

"We already have some promising youngsters. Players like Bob Nash, the outfielder we drafted from the Boston Red Sox organization; infielders Kevin Collin and Jim Lampe; outfielder Ron Swoboda, who impressed Casey with his slugging so much last spring; and pitchers like Mike Buist, Jerry Davey, Dennis Musgraves, Ron Locke and Jerry Hinsley. Some will develop, some won't. It's difficult to say which ones are more advanced. Each must be treated as an individual. I don't believe that a young ball player must always learn in the minor leagues. Sometimes a kid can learn more sitting on a major league bench. There's no set pattern.

"Our first objective, of course, will be to get out of the cellar. We don't intend to wait five years for that. When we start moving upward we won't look back. We'll make mistakes, sure, but we hope to keep them to a minimum. You can't except every rookie to make your ball club or every trade to work out perfectly."

Milestones, milestones, milestones! The Mets were always achieving them in one way or another. In the winter baseball meetings in Houston they found that Duke Carmel, a hard-hitting first baseman and outfielder on their Buffalo farm, had been drafted by—of all people—the Yankees. He cost them the $25,000 draft price and was the only player they went for among the senior-graded minor leaguers.

"Maybe they'll hafta' say some day that they started their comeback the day they drafted a Met," snorted Casey Stengel when he heard of it. "Now they're beginning to recognize us."

"I just had a physical exam," he continued, "an' now I'm set for the new season. There's nothing wrong with me except the usual fever. Now, wait a minute. This is a chronic fever. It comes from frustration. Maybe I'll just carry a thermometer around with me to see how high it gets."

Don Heffner, one of Casey's coaches, managed the Mets' St. Peterburg team in the Florida Winter League, assisted by Sheriff Robinson, another coach. He said he could understand Casey's frustration bit.

"The club finished second," he said. "Nothing much changed. We had about 30 kids, more than there were people in the stands some days. Nothing changed much. We kept losing."

The Mets' turnstiles were busier than New York's subway gates in 1964, when they chalked up the second largest attendance in the major leagues, with 2,547,549 customers admiring them, 1,732,597 at home. They wound up in the National League basement again, however. It marked the third straight cellar finish for Casey Stengel, who earlier won nine pennants in ten years as manager of the Yankees.

Despite the dismal showing, they set a record for the expansion club's brief history by winning 53 games. At the same time they became the first New York club ever to absorb 100 defeats for three straight years.

Losing 16 of their first 19 games, the Mets quickly became firmly entrenched in tenth place and never vacated the premises. They won only two out of 12 games in April, eight of 22 in June and seven out of 21 in September. Nevertheless fans swarmed to see them in shiny new Shea Stadium in fantastic numbers. As a result attendance rose 60 per cent over the 1963 draw at the crummy old Polo Grounds.

One of the brighter developments on the field was Joe Christopher's rise as a hitter. In five previous major league trials the young outfielder had never topped .263, but this time out he batted an even .300 and became the club's leading run producer with 76 RBIs.

Ron Hunt, boosting his average 31 points over the previous season, again was the club's top hitter with a .303 average, while Charlie Smith provided some bright moments by pacing the club with 20 home runs, though he batted only .239. Smith had been obtained from the Chicago White Sox shortly after the season began.

A disappointment was Al Jackson, the little lefthander

who had previously delivered such big efforts. Following a 13-victory mark in 1963, he was expected to better this mark. However, after breaking even in his first six games, he lost seven in a row and wound up with an 11–6 record. No other Met pitcher won more than ten games.

A spring training injury to Carl Willey jolted Stengel's pitching plans severely. The 33-year-old righthander suffered a multiple fracture of the jaw when he was struck by a line drive April 3. The mishap idled him until June 6. Subsequently Willey developed arm trouble and went through the season without winning a game, though he was in ten of them as a starting pitcher.

For the third straight year the Mets had a 20-game loser. This time it was Tracy Stallard, who dropped 20 decisions while winning ten.

Upward, ever upward, went the Mets' attendance records, but you couldn't say the same for their victory total. There was no improvement there. In fact, with 112 defeats compared to a mere 50 victories, they made their worst showing in 1965 since they first saw the light of day in 1962.

The misfortunes suffered by Ron Hunt dealt the club's chances of quitting the league basement a severe blow. A finger injury delayed the second baseman's debut until April 30. He had played just ten games when a separation of the left shoulder shelved him again. The injury, plus subsequent surgery, kept him out of the order until August 3.

An even more celebrated casualty was Casey Stengel. Returning from the Mets' Oldtimers party at Toots Shor's in the early hours of July 25, the septuagenarian manager suffered a fracture of the left hip when he fell getting out of a taxicab. Coach Wes Westrum ran the club that afternoon and on the following day was named interim manager for the remainder of the season.

In an attempt to improve the club with established performers, the Mets turned to a pair of veterans— pitcher Warren Spahn, 43, and catcher Yogi Berra, 39. Spahn won four of his first eight games, then dropped eight in a row before the club decided to release him July 12. Berra, signed as a coach, went on the active list April 27. However, after playing in only four games he decided to hang up the tools of his trade for good and let all those good Yankee years speak for his admittance to the Hall of Fame.

Not a single Metropolitan pitcher achieved double figures in the victory column this time. It was the first time a National League club failed to produce a ten-game winner since the Boston Braves and Philadelphia Phillies in 1945. Jack Fisher and Al Jackson led the staff with eight wins apiece, but Fisher lost 24 games and Jackson 20.

First Baseman Ed Kranepool led the club in hitting, though he batted a mere .253. Ron Swoboda, a rookie outfielder, was the home run leader with 19, but the 20-year-old youngster wasn't able to hit one after August 26.

They had one 11-game losing streak and another that went nine dreadful games and were never able to win more than three in a row. Their highest position was sixth place but that was in the first week in May and before the other clubs really got serious. They finished 47 games behind the pennant-winning Los Angeles Dodgers. Houston and Pittsburgh both beat them 14 times in 20 attempts. As mentioned, they looked good only at the gate, which showed that they played to a grand total of 2,843,820, of which 1,768,389 were Shea Stadium customers.

On August 30, Casey Stengel walked haltingly and with the aid of a cane to the end of a journey he began 55 years ago in Kankakee, Illinois.

In a gloomy press conference in a room off the lobby of the Essex House where he lived, the Professor announced his retirement as manager of the Mets.

"Right now I am not capable of walking out on the ball field," he said. "It's not proper for myself to limp out there. If I can't run out to take a pitcher out of the box, I don't wanna' complete my term."

The announcement was not unexpected. Yet it was not easy to realize it was the end or to imagine the baseball scene without him.

"I'll never forget the public here," said Casey, resuming his talk. "They've been very good to me."

He said he was truly sorry he hadn't guided the Mets out of last place but hoped he was leaving the nucleus of a better team behind.

"I believe I am leaving four or five players who will remain with the club ten or twelve years," he said.

He singled out Ron Hunt, Johnny Stephenson, Tug McGraw, Dennis Musgraves, Ron Swoboda and Roy McMillan for special praise.

"Swoboda will be here a long time," he said, "and you won't laugh at him next year. He can be a big man in baseball.

"I'd like to say a nice word about Mr. McMillan, my shortstop," he went on. "I thought maybe I booted one there when I got Weiss to pay fifty or sixty thousand dollars for him, but this season I've seen him do marvelous work. I think it's amazin' that this man did so well.

"Hunt has got what it takes to be a first division ball player. An' we got another young man who won three games for us with his hittin' an' he's only been playin' ball for a year an' a half.

"An' there's Christopher, who can be a mystery. Why, in the last eight days he's looked like Willie Mays hittin' all those home runs. He mustn't have known that fence was out there to hit home runs over all season."

He also praised Westrum. "He's done a wonderful job," said Casey: "He has the men playin' aggressive baseball. An' of course you know how good the coaches are."

He looked across at his wife Edna, who was showing reporters a replica of the steel ball that was planted in Casey's hip during the operation.

"In all his years in baseball nobody has treated Casey as well as the Mets," Edna said. "Everything works out for the best. I know Casey hates to give up that uniform. I don't know what that feels like. I've never had a uniform."

His old Yankees were playing games on the West Coast but they made themselves heard.

"I hope he stays in baseball," said Whitey Ford, "just because he likes it so much an' because he's such a great guy even though he used to get a lot of players mad at him. . . ."

"He gave me the greatest break of my career," said Tony Kubek. "George Weiss and Lee MacPhail wanted to keep me in the minors for more experience, but Casey kept me as a utility man and I played 40 games.

"He sent me a check for $25 when I got married. He said he didn't know what to buy.

"My wife and I were on the way to the church and I realized I didn't have any money. We stopped in a drug store and the druggist was about to cash the check when he saw Casey's signature. He asked if he could keep the check as a souvenir.

"I told him that would goof up Casey's checkbook, but I'd write Casey and ask his permission. Casey wrote back to say it would be all right. He also said a drugstore was a funny place to be spending a wedding present."

Wes Westrum took a calculated risk in accepting the interim manager's job when Casey was hospitalized. He had everything to gain and little to lose. He took a definite stand.

"We've looked at the old players for four years," he said. "We've got nothing to lose giving the kids a chance."

What Westrum had to lose was a substantial number of ball games, of course, if the kids failed. It could result in his dropping out of the running for the job when Casey decided to quit.

Under Westrum the Mets won 19 and lost 48 (Casey's record for the season was 31–64). He gave the player development program priority over a won-and-lost record. The results of this decision were underscored by the emergence of 21-year-old Tug McGraw and 22-year-old Dick Selma as two of the most promising pitching prospects in the major leagues, and of 23-year-old Darrell Sutherland as a relief jobber of top quality.

A stocky 43-year-old of Norwegian extraction, Westrum was born and raised in the rugged lake and lumber country of Clearbrook, Minnesota. He excelled as a football fullback and basketball guard in high school. The eldest of four children, he went into professional baseball at the age of 17 as a means of helping support a widowed mother.

His entire major league playing career was with the Giants as a catcher. He was a key figure on two National League championship teams, including the 1951 club that accomplished the "Miracle of Coogan's Bluff" by winning the pennant in a playoff with the Dodgers after being 13½ games out of first place as late as August 11. The 1954 Giants swept the World Series against the Cleveland Indians with Wes behind the plate.

After his playing career came to an end under Bill Rigney after the San Francisco Giant's 1957 campaign, Wes became one of the club's coaches.

A rare coaching trade brought him to the Mets. It happened after the 1963 season, when Harry (Cookie) Lavagetto, then on Stengel's staff, was stricken by illness. When Lavagetto expressed a desire to return to his native San Francisco area, Stengel and Weiss arranged with Horace Stoneham, the Giants' president, to exchange coaches.

If the Mets had any chance at all of making it out of the cellar in the 1966 season such prospects were in new manager Westrum's hands.

APPROACHING MEDIOCRITY

When Wes Westrum was reappointed manager for 1966, M. Donald Grant, the Chairman of the Board, said:

"Westrum has justified our every confidence in his ability to bring about immediate improvement in the Mets and develop a field and clubhouse attitude that encourages high promise for the future."

By the time the 1966 season had ended Westrum had measured up to every word. He directed the Mets to the greatest number of victories (66) in their history, lifted the club for the first time from last place, and held true to his promise by putting an exciting hit-and-run attack into operation.

The mute figures were eloquent testimony to the latter: the stolen base output was increased from 28 to 55. But more than that, his positive approach, supplemented by a gifted eye of observation, enabled the Mets to reduce their frustrating strikeout total from 1,129 to 992 (or almost one per game), while raising their team batting average from .221 to .239.

However, the Mets fell back to their old losing habits in 1967. Finishing 28 games behind in his first season, they started poorly and finished worse, winding up in last place again, 40½ games out of first place. Westrum resigned in mid-September, with Salty Parker, the third base coach, being named the interim manager.

Just as they did in 1967, the Mets finished the 1968 season without a manager. Gil Hodges succumbed to chest pains while managing the club in Atlanta on September 24. He was rushed to a hospital where it was learned that he had suffered a mild heart attack. His close friend and pitching coach, Rube Walker, handled the club in the final five games.

Despite reassuring words from the doctors that Hodges' heart attack was a mild one, there was an obvious pall cast over the most successful season in the Mets' history. Even before he suffered his heart attack, Hodges had led the club to his goal of 70 wins, four more than any Met team had ever registered. In the end the Mets won 73, lost only 89. They finished ninth, same as they did under Westrum in 1966, but their won-lost record this time was much better.

Financially the club did pretty good too. Despite their ninth-place finish the Mets drew 1,781,657 paying customers into Shea Stadium. It was the second highest attendance in club history.

The Mets, who once were the laugh of the league, became the talk of the league with their fine young pitching staff. When the season began and the Mets got one strong game after another from the likes of Tom Seaver, Jerry Koosman, Nolan Ryan and Don Cardwell, the experts wondered how long it would last. It lasted all year, to the astonishment of everyone. The Mets led the league most of the season with an earned run average around two runs a game. It wasn't until the last two or three weeks that the pennant-winning St. Louis Cardinals dipped below them. In the end, the Mets finished fourth with an ERA of .272. But they were second in shutouts with 25, surpassed only by the Cardinals, who had 30.

Koosman, a rookie lefthander, was the biggest surprise. He came from nowhere to win 19 games, seven of them shutouts. He completed half of his 34 starts. Seaver, who was Rookie of the Year in 1967, duplicated his freshman season with 10 victories and a 2.20 ERA.

Dick Selma, Jim McAndrew and Ryan contributed greatly. Selma at one point won six in a row. McAndrew, after losing his first five—four of them in which the Mets failed to score a run for him—finished with a 4–7 record. He didn't join the Mets until July 21, so all his good work was done down the stretch after Ryan faded.

Hodges established the Mets as a solid team. He wanted none of the shuttling back and forth that went on in 1967 when they used a total of 54 players. Under Hodges, they employed only 34.

Other than the pitching the biggest surprise was catcher Jerry Grote, who hit .300 through the first half of the season and was selected as a catcher on the All Star team.

Their No. I hitter was Cleon Jones at .297. Ed Charles also had a fine year. The veteran third baseman led the club in homers with 15, drove in 53 runs and batted a respectable .276. However, with a team batting average of .228, the Mets had the weakest attack in the league.

THE YEAR OF THE TIGER

A lot of people felt sorry for Hodges and the Mets as they went through the motions in spring training. The manager talked optimistically about their 1969 chances but not many took them seriously.

Some checked out of Florida wondering if Gil, just then recovering from a heart attack, would be able to survive a last-place finish by his club.

Jerry Koosman and Tom Seaver, the big young winners of the year before, didn't look good at all. Koosman had an ailing arm and Seaver was being bombed regularly in exhibition games. Bud Harrelson, the shortstop, hadn't played in a game because of a knee which was slow to respond to therapy following surgery, and in general prospects looked bleak.

Those astute gentlemen, the price-makers, considered everything and made it 25 to 1 against the Mets winning in the Eastern Division and 100 to 1 against them getting to the World Series. In the pre-season odds the St. Louis

Cardinals were made 2 to 5 to win the East and Chicago 3 to 1.

Oh there was one good omen present before the season started, but because of the Mets' past behavior few people paid any attention to it. The augury was a very inside thing. The club that won the Florida Instructional League title was sure to win the following summer. In 1965 the Baltimore Orioles won the Florida Instructional League—where young players were tried and developed and older ones sought to sharpen up for one more whirl —and the next season they became world champions. The Boston Red Sox won the FIL title in 1966 and won the 1967 American League pennant (at odds of 100 to 1) and they chased the St. Louis Cardinals to the seventh game of the World Series. In 1967 the Detroit Tigers won the FIL championship and the parent club went on in 1968 to win its first American League bunting in 23 years. Last year the Mets' instructional league team beat out a dozen others.

Then, slowly, sometimes unexpectedly, things began to happen. Working effectively with Coach Rube Walker and delegating a lot of responsibility to him, Hodges set up a five-man pitching staff consisting of Seaver, Koosman, Don Cardwell, Nolan Ryan and Gary Gentry, with veteran righthander Kal Koonce and young lefthander Tug McGraw the leading relief specialists.

The pitching staff, well rested at every turn and handled well by Walker and Hodges, became the best in the league and remained potent when the arms on other clubs began to show wear and tear.

In the beginning Cleon Jones was the lone outfield regular, then Tommie Agee, who had been benched in the early going, found himself. Harrelson took over at shortstop for keeps. Jerry Grote began to catch very professional games regularly. Hodges began to platoon his troops effectively and efficiently.

Ed Charles, 35 years old, was too old to play regularly and not show his age. Hodges spelled him with young Wayne Garrett and together they gave the Mets fine third base play. He platooned Al Weis, Art Shamsky, Donn Clendenon, Ken Boswell, Rod Gaspar and others.

Clendenon's presence was the result of a master move by John Murphy, the architect of the Mets. On June 15, after considerable maneuvering, he obtained the long-ball hitting first baseman from Montreal. Donn made the club better with his power. He made Ed Kranepool better with his presence. With the two of them available the club now had one fine first baseman.

Once, early in the going, Hodges got off the bench, walked out to Jones and removed him from left field because he thought the outfielder hadn't hustled enough on a drive. On May 15 the manager made another move along the same lines.

The Mets had lost a game to Atlanta because of what Gil considered sloppy baseball, the kind they used to play regularly. They trudged into the clubhouse afterwards ready for their usual beer. They got no beer. They got hell instead.

Hodges told them they were professionals and they were never to forget it. They were men. They should stop playing like kids, making mistakes, dreaming of before and after the game pleasures. He told them they could take their laziness to the Tidewater farm club. He put the message across.

"We needed that," said Boswell afterwards. "We stopped thinking finishing third would be a good year. He told us to start thinking about finishing first."

"The best thing about it," said McGraw, "is that he never raised his voice and he never mentioned names."

That's when the Mets started growing up. They had

achieved respectability of sorts earlier in the season when they won four out of six games from the league-leading Cubs, two at Shea and then, a week later, two in Chicago, but they hadn't taken themselves too seriously. On August 15 they were 9½ games behind the first place Cubs in the Eastern Division.

Then came the change. From that date through the final victory over the Baltimore Orioles in the World Series they were winners, particularly in Shea Stadium. They won 26 out of 31 games there for a percentage of .839. Their pitchers gave up only six home runs in their last 253 innings played at Shea, a remarkable accomplishment since their home park is considered by home run hitters as a kindly successor to the Mets' old home, the Polo Grounds.

When the Cubs arrived at Shea for a two-game series in September, their margin had been cut to 2½ games and their mood was grim in contrast to their carefree approach to things in earlier games with the Mets.

In retrospect the first pitch thrown by Bill Hands, the Cubs' starting pitcher in the first game, to lead-off batter Tommie Agee, decided the course of events for the Mets during the next seven days. It was an intimidating pitch.

"I don't mind that," Agee had said at the time, "as long as we retaliate."

They did. On his first pitch of the game Jerry Koosman hit Chicago slugger Ron Santo on the arm. The Mets had stood their ground. Agee hit a two-run homer and a double his next two times at bat and slid around Catcher Randy Hundley to score the winning run in a 3–2 Met victory.

The following night Tom Seaver held the Cubs at bay while the Mets mistreated pitcher Ferguson Jenkins. They got two runs in the first inning and the duel was over, but they went on to win 7–1 and the Cubs' once proud 9½-game lead was down to a lowly half game.

Early the next evening the Mets, by virtue of having won a 12-inning game from Montreal in the first half of a twi-night double-header, moved into first place on percentage points. When they won the second game too while Chicago was losing in Philadelphia, the Mets were on top for the first time in their history.

Mrs. Joan Payson, the Mets' owner, stepped down from her box next to the home dugout and walked toward home plate with tears in her eyes. Then she turned back and went to the elevators in the back of the Stadium.

"How does it feel?" asked an irrepressible radio man.

"Great," was the classic reply.

"What are you going to do to relax?"

"I'm going upstairs to have a drink," she said.

She wasn't alone.

The Mets held on to their lead and won the championship of the Eastern division going away, like any true Thoroughbred. The night they clinched the pennant, September 24, with a 6–0 win over St. Louis at Shea, was a night to remember, on a par with VJ day or at least the repeal of prohibition. When Gary Gentry retired the last Cardinal, the fans spilled out of the stands and turned the playing area into the Flushing version of the running of the bulls at Pamplona. Everybody—the new breed, the kooks, the banner-makers, the disillusioned Giants and Dodger fans, the jet-setters who had decided the Mets were "in"—all took to the field and did their thing. Their "thing" amounted to a spontaneous dance for joy in honor of the new heroes—the Amazing Mets.

When the play-off for the National League championship began in Atlanta the Mets again looked familiar. They were the underdogs. But again they ignored the odds in a three-game sweep that sent the experts to their couches.

When they needed hitting they got it. When they needed pitching it was there. When situations called for infallible decisions Hodges was there to make them.

In two of the three games the Braves held leads. But the pitching that had carried them to ten straight victories and 17 wins in 20 games during their drive to the National League's Western Division title could not handle the Mets' sudden power in the clutch.

The Met starters didn't finish any of the games but Hodges was always able to find the solution in his bullpen. In the first game, which Seaver began, Ron Taylor pitched two shutout innings to end the game. In the second, started by Koosman, Taylor and McGraw combined for 4½ shutout innings. And in the finale, Ryan, taking over for Gentry in the third inning, allowed three hits the rest of the way to pick up a 7–4 win that made the Amazins the National League champions.

Seaver, who hadn't done much running in the outfield before his start because of a pulled leg muscle, said he didn't quite have his good stuff.

"When most other pitchers don't have their good stuff, you brace yourself for line drives," said Harrelson. "But when Seaver doesn't have it you figure he'll beat them anyway."

"There's no telling what these guys can do," said Koosman. "They gave me an eight-run lead and I let most of it get away. But they didn't let it bother them a bit. They went out and got some more.

"Sitting around during the long innings while we were scoring those runs hurt," Jerry continued. "My control went awry. I couldn't get the curve over for a strike and they started waiting for the fastball. It's kind of embarrassing blowing a big lead but we won and I'll accept it."

"I'll tell you," said Paul Richards, general manager of the Braves, "they way the Mets are going they might sweep the Orioles too. I haven't seen Hodges make a wrong move all year. Bringing in Ryan in the third inning was a helluva move."

Hodges had pulled Ryan out of the bullpen to replace Gentry with runners on second and third, none out and Rico Carty, a dangerous batter, hitting at a one-ball, two-strike count.

"I had no idea what I was going to do when I left the dugout," said Gil afterwards. "But I knew it was a touchy situation and we needed a strikeout, maybe two of them."

Ryan made his first pitch one of his best. It was a fastball over the outside corner. Carty swung and missed. Hodges had one of his strikeouts. After the manager ordered an intentional base on balls to Orlando Cepeda, Ryan struck out Clete Boyer on four pitches. Then Bob Dider popped up and it was over.

Hank Aaron, the Atlanta slugger, had high regard for the Mets when it was all over.

"Every time they had to win they won for the past month," he said. "I'm sure they can beat Baltimore in the Series. They've got the pitching. I've been batting against Seaver and Koosman for two and three years and I know they've got the stuff."

After the win that won the pennant the fans again went wild on the field, tearing up the infield sod, making away with home plate and the bases and milling around the place for hours.

In their clubhouse the Mets made the earlier celebration after gaining first place seem like a church clambake. They bathed in champagne before drinking any of it. Gary Gentry plastered Jerry Grote in the face with a mutual birthday cake. Rod Gaspar sloshed a bottle of the bubbly over the head of Mayor John Lindsay, who sputtered, "I love it," then took the bottle and gave Gaspar a shower.

"Hey Mayor, you shoulda been here last week," yelled Seaver, to Lindsay, visiting in the middle of a mayoralty campaign.

Lindsay winced. People are always saying things like that to politicians.

Over in a corner, Ed Charles, poet-laureate of the club, was singing "East Side, West Side," his battle song for the Amazin's.

In the bars of Manhattan, Brooklyn, Queens, the Bronx and elsewhere celebrations took on a New Year's Eve bedlam. In George Tansey's Jade Room in Fort Lee, N.J., a hot-bed of Mets fans despite the town's closeness to Yankee Stadium, a banner hung over the bar reading:

"Seave and Koos and bring on the booze."

THE IMPOSSIBLE DREAM

Days before Baltimore met with the Mets in the first game of the World Series, Frank Robinson had stepped onto a chair in the middle of a celebrating bunch of Orioles, and shouted:

"Ron Gasper has just said on television that the Mets will sweep us in four games. Bring on Ron Gasper, whoever the hell he is. . . . Quiet! I've just been told that his name is Rod Gaspar, whoever the hell *he* is."

In his own way Robinson was letting it be known that he didn't think too much of the Mets. Apparently the majority of the baseball handicappers went along with him because the American Leaguers were 8 to 5 favorites in the best four-out-of-seven competition. Odds-makers said they couldn't remember an American League team so heavily favored since the Yankees were in their glory.

The Orioles were, indeed, being favorably compared to the great Yankee teams of 1927, 1932 and 1939, with Babe Ruth, Lou Gehrig, Tony Lazzeri, Bill Dickey and

Joe DiMaggio, and 1961, whey they had Mickey Mantle and Roger Maris. Also with Connie Mack's fabled Philadelphia Athletics of 1929 and 1931 with the Million Dollar Infield.

Equipped with fine power hitters like Frank Robinson, Boog Powell, Brooks Robinson and Paul Blair, they also could boast of the best pitching staff in the American League. And on defense they could be highly recommended with the left side of the infield (Brooks Robinson at third and Mark Belanger at shortstop) one of the best baseball had ever seen.

Frank Lane, considered one of the smartest men in the game, was asked if he considered the Mets a team of destiny.

Lane, who now happens to be a Baltimore scout, answered: "Indeed I do. I believed they are destined to be beaten easily by the Orioles.

Lum Harris was one of the many managers who didn't go along with the theory that the Mets could make more magic. He said so right after the New Yorkers rubbed out his Atlanta Braves in three straight games.

"I don't believe them," he said. "How can I? I don't know how they do it. All I know is that they are in the World Series instead of us and I never thought it would happen.

"All I know is that things like that weren't happening to the Mets early in the season. No broken-bat hits, no line drives sticking in the webbing of their gloves. No home runs over the centerfield fence and no one coming in from the bullpen to strike out the side."

The Orioles were busy trying to learn as much as possible about the Mets before the World Series began, primarily from reports drawn up by Jim Russo and Al Kubski, the Oriole scouts who in more recent weeks studied the New York *wünderkind* more closely than space scientists were examining rocks from the moon.

Russo was the man who was given much of the credit for the Orioles' easy success—a four game sweep—over the Los Angeles Dodgers in the 1966 World Series.

Because of the manner in which the Mets wiped out Atlanta in the play-offs, however, it was conceded that the scouting study might show something different from what the Orioles had been led to expect—a report emphasizing good pitching and questionable hitting. In fact Weaver, commenting on the Mets' play during the play-offs, once said: "Are they trying to confuse our scouts? They sure surprised us."

But the manager added, "I really don't know much about them. I knew a lot of their players in the minor leagues but I don't know how they've changed.

"We didn't play the Mets any exhibition games last spring," he added. "But when we played them last year Seaver and Koosman pitched against us. Seaver has always thrown strikes any time I've seen him. Koosman had to struggle in the minors but he looked good against us in that spring training game.

"Neither of them throws as hard as Jim Palmer, for velocity with the fast ball alone. Palmer has to rank with the fastest ones.

"Tommie Agee has progressed and matured since I saw him in the minors. He hadn't learned how to put the bat on the ball consistently. I know Boswell is a slap hitter and Ron Swoboda had a lot of holes to pitch to. That was in the minors, though. I don't know as much about them now."

The World Series was only a few minutes old before the Mets woke up and realized that life wasn't all Scotch and soda. Don Buford, the Orioles' lead-off man, hit Tom Seaver's second pitch over the bright green canvas wall in right field. Ron Swoboda made a hysterical spread-eagle leap for the ball and missed, a hint that the Mets' mystique would be impotent that day.

It was. Going about their chores in a businesslike manner the American League champions artfully compiled a 4–1 triumph in the opening game before 50,249 in Baltimore's Municipal Stadium.

The Mets were sternly gripped by Mike Cuellar, a lefthander with an effective screwball. He allowed six hits, not more than two to any inning, and was helped out of his only jam on a sensational play by third baseman Brooks Robinson in the seventh inning.

The Mets didn't look or sound as though they thought a four-game sweep by the Orioles, predicted by some, was on the way, however. In the clubhouse afterwards, Seaver, Clendenon, Jones, all had the same line: "We'll win it in five."

Seaver wasn't shocked by Buford's homer, though he couldn't remember anyone hitting a lead-off blast against him before. He threw Buford a high inside pitch, which the Mets' scouts advised, and could later giggle: "Gee but those USC guys have fast bats." Both Seaver and Buford are Southern California grads.

What troubled Seaver was his fourth inning fatigue. "I ran out of gas," he said. "My zip died. I told Rube [pitching coach Rube Walker] 'I'm losing it.' I'll be ready for 'em in four days, though, believe me."

"Bring on Ron Gasper," yelled Frank Robinson, giving the Baltimore battle cry—and getting the name wrong again.

The second game baseball—and a great deal more— was in Jerry Koosman's hands. It developed that they were very good hands indeed. Because he pitched brilliantly—a no-hitter for six innings, a two-hitter into the ninth—the Mets were able to outlast the Orioles, 2-1.

After a fourth-inning home run by Don Clendenon, they found themselves beating the favored American Leaguers with Al Weis, a .215 hitter; Ron Taylor, the last-out relief pitcher; and Ed Charles, the 36-year-old third baseman.

There were other, prettier helpers too. After the Orioles had used seventh-inning singles by Paul Blair and Brooks Robinson—their only hits of the afternoon—and Blair's stolen base to push across the tying run, there was a sudden commotion in one right-field aisle. There four of the stronger sex were parading down the Baltimore aisles with "Let's Go Mets" painted in shoe-black on a hotel bedsheet.

They were the Mets' wives, led by Nancy Seaver, Lynn Dyer, Ruth Ryan and Melanie Pfeil. The Oriole fans pelted them with peanuts, which was no way to treat a lady, to say nothing of four of them, all pretty.

The Mets had scored first in the fourth on Clendenon's home run. The winning run, and practically all of the drama, came in the ninth. There were two out when Charles singled and, running with the pitch, made third on a single into left field by Jerry Grote. On the next pitch Weis hit Dave McNally's high slider into left field for the deciding run.

Weis, the quiet supersub of the Met infield, had hit only 40 singles during the regular season and two home runs, both against Chicago.

"Had it been any other manager I believe I would have been taken out for a pinch-hitter," he said softly. "Gil has stayed with me and I'm thankful."

In the Baltimore ninth Koosman was trying to protect the 2-1 lead Weis had given him. With two out he walked Frank Robinson and Boog Powell, both on 3-2 counts. Hodges took him out and made the veteran Ron

Taylor the relief jobber.

Robinson pounded a 3 and 2 pitch behind third base. It might have been a hit had not Charles been playing him deep.

"I tried to get to third but the runner was practically there," said Charles. "But Brooks is not the fastest thing on foot and I knew that I could get him at first." He did with a throw that Clendenon dug out of the dirt and it was the Mets' game.

"Did you know that your home run put the Orioles behind for the first time in any post-season game?" said a man in charge of esoteric trivia.

"Good," grunted Clendenon, law student, restaurateur and vice president of Scripto Inc. "I hope they get used to it."

Now it was time for the change to Shea Stadium. Some wondered how the Orioles would adjust to the hysteria there. Were they ready for that ear-blasting, bedsheet waving bird cage on the Flushing Flats?

Catcher Clay Dalrymple, one of the few Orioles who had savored the terrors there, wasn't so sure.

"It's hard to prepare for the bedlam there," said the former National Leaguer. "The cutoff men won't be able to hear, the outfielders won't hear each other, and it's all distracting. It's like going from a quiet room into a circus tent. I've talked about it and I'll tell 'em again."

Tommie Agee's spectacular fielding and his big bat led the Mets to a 5–0 decision, witnessed by 56,335 wildly happy fans. They seemed to realize for the first time that the Orioles, doubtless a very fine team, could be had by the Mets.

Agee hit a lead-off homer off Jim Palmer in the first inning, then twice robbed the Baltimores of extra-base hits.

Behind 3–0, the Orioles started what looked like a big rally in the fourth inning by putting two runners on with two out and Elrod Hendricks at bat. Normally a lefthanded pull hitter, Hendricks hit a pitch to deep left center. Agee, shaded to the right, went galloping after the ball and caught it with a backhanded catch two steps from the fence to end the inning. Three innings later after an even longer run he dove to rescue a potential triple with the bases loaded. On defense he made a difference of five runs, and on offense, one with his homer.

Agee had led off the Mets first with a homer. The second inning was even more productive for the Mets. With two out Jerry Grote walked and Bud Harrelson singled. This brought up Gary Gentry, who had driven in only one run in 74 times-at-bat during the season. Once again that ethereal something called Met-icism came through. Gentry promptly drove in two runs with a double. It was his first hit since August 3.

Gentry, one week past his twenty-third birthday, had turned suddenly wild in the fourth, causing Hodges to bring Nolan Ryan, 22-year-old hero of the last play-off game, to the mound. After Agee helped him with his fantastic catch on Blair, he turned in a magnificent relief job until the ninth when the Orioles loaded the bases with two out. Behind the dangerous Blair 0 and 2, the youngster switched from his fastball to breaking stuff, and at 2 and 2 broke a curve over the plate. Blair was caught looking and Shea Stadium was caught up in one tremendous roar.

Brooks Robinson met a Tom Seaver fastball solidly and drove it on a low line toward right center field and suddenly everything seemed in order for the 1969 World Series. Baltimore was getting the clutch hits again. The

Mets seemed to be reeling under all that pressure. Two
runs would surely score and the Orioles would win the
fourth game and even the series at 2–2.

Then large Ron Swoboda charged into the picture.
Instead of trying to cut the ball off on a bounce and
salvage one run, he went headlong after it, risking everything to make a diving catch.

It worked. He somehow managed to snare the ball in
the webbing of his glove just before his face hit the
grass. He lurched to his feet and threw home. One run
scored but disaster had been averted. The Orioles had
only tied the game in the ninth instead of going ahead
and now they were the ones with spinning heads.

In the tenth inning Baltimore's Don Buford lost a
fly ball in the sun and turned it into a double. The
Orioles, now afraid of the suddenly fearsome Al Weis,
walked him intentionally. Pinch-hitter J. C. Martin
bunted. Catcher Elrod Hendricks called for it but in the
hysterical din of Shea fans, pitcher Pete Richert couldn't
hear him. He grabbed the ball, threw hurriedly to first
and hit Martin on the wrist. The ball rolled toward second and the game was the Mets' 2–1.

"It was beautiful to watch them chase that ball," said
Swoboda. "It looked like a Chinese fire drill."

Next day the Orioles launched a desperate bid to
overcome the Mets' three-games-to-one lead in the Series.
They scored three runs off lefthander Jerry Koosman,
who had beaten them in the second game. Mark Belanger
singled, Pitcher Dave McNally homered and Frank
Robinson hit one into the stands. For the first time in
the Series the Mets fell behind in a game they were
destined to win.

The Mets finally got on the scoreboard in the sixth.
Cleon Jones skipped to get out of the way of one of
McNally's low curves. The ball rocketed into the New

York dugout as plate umpire Lou DiMuro called it a ball.

Jones protested that he had been hit on the foot by the ball. When Hodges retrieved the ball and showed that it was marked with a black smudge of shoe polish, incontrovertable evidence that he had been struck by the pitch, DiMuro waved Jones to first base.

"We always keep three or four balls smudged with shoe polish in the dugout,' Casey Stengel cracked afterwards.

Donn Clendenon then drove the ball to the face of the scoreboard in left field and the Mets trailed by only one run, 3–2. The homer was the third in the Series by Clendenon, one shy of the record held by Babe Ruth, Lou Gehrig, Hank Bauer and Duke Snider.

Before departing for a pinch-hitter in the eighth, Mc-Nally yielded a second homer, one that dripped with even more historical significance than Clendenon's drive.

Leading off the seventh Al Weis drove the ball over the 371-foot mark in left field for another homer to tie the score. In the platooned second baseman's two seasons with the Mets, 212 homers were hit at Shea Stadium but none by Weis. It was his fifth Series hit, giving him a .455 average in 11 trips to the plate.

It didn't take long after that. With Eddie Watt pitching in McNally's place, Jones doubled to lead off the eight. Clendenon then grounded out. With first base open the Orioles could have walked slugger Swoboda intentionally but they decided to pitch to him. He lined the ball to left field and Jones scored the run that put the Mets in front 4–3. One out later Boog Powell mishandled Jerry Grote's grounder and Swoboda scored the Mets' fifth run.

All that remained was for Koosman to dispose of three Orioles in the ninth and fantasy would become reality.

Frank Robinson opened with a walk, but Powell and Brooks Robinson were easy outs. When Jones grabbed Dave Johnson's soft fly it was all over, 5–3, and there sat the Mets, atop Mount Olympus.

In the clubhouse, bedlam. Afterwards the Mets and visitors took their now usual champagne shower.

"This is the summit!" shouted Ed Charles. "We're No. 1 in the world and you can't just get any bigger than this."

"Some people might not believe in us," said Cleon Jones, "but then some people still think the world is flat."

"It boiled down to this," chimed in Bud Harrelson. "When it had to be done we did it and they didn't."

"We're the saints of lost causes," yelled Ron Swoboda. "We've done it all. The only thing left to do is go to the moon."

In the middle of the room stood Judge Sam Liebo-witz. "At this moment," he said, "I will even forgive Walter O'Malley for leaving Brooklyn for Los Angeles." He paused. "Almost," he said.

"I predicted we'd take four straight," said Jerry Koosman, the man who won the second game and now had won the last. "I didn't say we'd win the first four, just four straight and we did. My wife says from now on she'll believe anything I say."

They called Hodges to the telephone and told him President Nixon was calling from the White House.

Gil listened a few minutes, smiling happily, then said: "Thank you Mr. President, thank you very much. Good-bye sir, and God bless you."

In the middle of the revelry, Tug McGraw walked up to Koosman with an apple tucked between his chin and his chest, the symbol of the chockup, and said:

"I'm from Baltimore and I just want to say hello."

The rest of the Mets got the gag.

Don Cardwell picked up little Al Weis and yelled, "If this one isn't voted the Most Valuable Player, the sports-writers are drunk."

Clendenon was voted the star of the series, thus winning a 1970 Dodge presented by *Sport* Magazine. Asked if he thought it was the proper choice, Hodges said, "Let's see, how many cars should be given out? Make it 29—25 players who were all heroes and four fine coaches. The manager doesn't need a car. He has one."

"This was a team affair all the way," he went on. "When did I begin to think we'd get into the play-offs and maybe the World Series? In May and June when we won 11 straight. That was the high point. We began to be a ball club then.

"This bunch has the makings of one big happy family, the way the Dodgers were in Brooklyn for ten wonderful years. I'd like to see something like that."

He called it bigger and better than any of his seven World Series as a Dodger player.

"It's because I'm the manager in this one," he said, then quickly added, lest the wrong interpretation be given to his words. "It's because of the kind of a team this is. The Dodgers went into every World Series as a class team. This one was never thought of like that."

Hodges' family finally made their way into his office abaft the main dressing room. The first was Gil Jr., the college student, who hastily climbed out of his business suit and into his Met uniform for the occasion. Then came his mother and his daughters and Joan Hodges, his wife.

A moment later, when the head of the family entered, Joan Hodges, who had lived through her husband's triumphs and setbacks with such fervor all these years, cried:

"You know what we are? You know? We're champions of the world. Imagine, we did it."

Hodges hugged her back, and his daughters. Then Gil Jr. put his arms around them from behind while a photographer snapped a family portrait.

Casey Stengel entered and shook his hand. Then Gil sat down and tried to match Casey's non-stop monologue.

"You done the best job anybody ever did in baseball," he said to Gil. "You and your coaches and players are just wonderful. You got Saboda [Casey still had trouble pronouncing the outfielder's name] good, an' you got Jones good and this is the only club that don't have to rebuild, an' you got 'em."

"Casey, you got it all started," Hodges said. "You gave them confidence in the beginning and it all started with you and they couldn't have done it if you hadn't been there first . . . and I can't keep it up because I can't talk like you."

Yogi Berra, the coach, who was in so many of them with the Yankees, was overjoyed at this Series victory.

"I told you in June these kids had it," he said. "They never stopped believing in themselves."

Shouted Rod Gaspar: "Bring on Frank Robinson— whoever he is."

Tom Seaver hugged everybody until he was spent. Gary Gentry grabbed the pitcher in his locker and said loudly, "Everybody leave Seav alone. Seav doesn't want to talk anymore."

But Seaver, the personable, articulate young pitching star of the year, lit a long cigar and leaned on a white trash can by his locker, watching the mad scene, and when someone walked over he began talking as if to himself.

"I just want to watch this and listen," he said. "I want to absorb it, so I'll remember it the rest of my life. I keep saying the words, 'World Champions,' but I won't believe it until Christmas. I hope people outside this team felt what was happening inside with us, what we really did. . . . I mean, I hope 200 million people felt it. It shows what men can do together."

Upstairs in the press room Nancy Seaver, pert, blond, blue-eyed wife of the pitcher, was busy at a typewriter. She had been signed to write a daily column during the Series for the New York *Post*. She wrote things like:

"Every four days my husband stops speaking to me.

"It's not the kind of thing that makes me want to start packing my bags for Juarez, but it creates some pretty weird problems.

"Tom starts getting pretty preoccupied with things like the pattern of the kitchen wallpaper on the night before he pitches. By the day of the game he's in a mental world of his own.

"That's when the fun starts.

" 'George,' I'll say. That's his name you know, George Thomas Seaver. 'George, how do you like the new collar I bought for Slider?' Slider's our dog. 'George?' 'George?'

"Then he'll say something like, 'Can't you see I'm reading, Nancy?'

"Sure enough, he'll have his nose buried in *The Grapes of Wrath*. Only the pages don't turn. What's turning are those little wheels and sprockets.

"From then on, we speak in a sort of code. I've learned to rely on my own special brand of E.S.P. to break the code and find out just what's going on behind those grunts and pregnant pauses."

Commented Ike Gellis, sports editor of the *Post:* "She does a better job than a lot of writers. And I *know* she's a lot prettier."

When most of the mob had left Hodges' hut in the clubhouse, Johnny Murphy, the Mets' general manager,

came in to add his congratulations. Gil returned the
compliment, for the deals for Tommie Agee, Al Weis,
Donn Clendenon, and others, as well as the deals he
refused to make, had much to do with the club's success.

As one of the game's greatest relief pitchers as a
Yankee, the one-time "Fordham Fireman" hated to give
up a run. As a general manager Murphy hated to give
up kid pitchers. The Shea Stadium midsummer madness
would not have happened had Murphy bitten for one
of the offers for his wunderkinds. Such as:

In March the St. Louis Cardinals almost wrapped up
a multiplayer deal that would have included the Mets'
Nolan Ryan, the relief hero, for Joe Torre. Murphy
backed off.

The Phillies made a pitch to deliver Richie Allen to
the Mets. They wanted Tom Seaver or Jerry Koosman,
but came down to such names as Gary Gentry, Jim Mc-
Andrew, Amos Otis and Jon Matlock (then still in the
minors). Again, no dice.

The Baltimore Orioles pressed him to take Frank
Robinson for either Seaver or Koosman. Murphy turned
it down.

Hodges knew about the offers. "You build with pitching," he said. "We didn't give up any of those good
young ones."

"The club played inspired ball in the play-offs and in
the World Series," said Murphy. "Those are the things
that won. But one year doesn't make a dynasty as someone suggested. We're not in any such category. We
realize it took hard work and spirit and luck and that's
what it will take again."

Outside on the playing field there was a familiar scene.
Once again thousands of delirious fans had poured on
the field eager for plunder. They again sacked the
Stadium, making away with bases and tearing up the

sod. Kids all over town that night walked around with big rolls of greed sod like crazy ponchos over their heads.

"Hey," shouted a cop at Times Square that night to a group of young celebrants. "You guys are wearing the whole damn Met outfield."

Afterwards the club held a victory celebration upstairs in the Diamond Club. There were celebrities. Pearl Bailey, wearing a big "Go Mets" button and a big tuft of grass from the Shea playing surface, gave Ed Charles a big kiss and shouted, "There, that'll make you play 18 more years."

The players grouped in the middle of the room and sang, "You gotta Have Heart," and then, "God Bless America."

The party went on and on. Someone offered to bet that the Great Western champagne people would need a new vineyard. The Mets were again batting 1.000 against the bubbly.

The following Monday they held a heroes parade and reception for the Mets and it proved bigger and noisier than any before. Some said in advance that a city that had been apparently drained of every happy emotion following the Mets' amazing World Series victory Thursday couldn't possibly rise to the occasion with the same lusty outpouring of admiration and joy. But they underestimated New Yorkers even as they had underestimated the Mets.

From the Battery to City Hall to Bryant Park and later to Flushing Meadow Park and Shea Stadium, where they were the guests of those other world champions, the football Jets, hundreds of thousands of exultant worshipers poured out their tributes to Hodges and his men.

Hodges and his wife Joan rode in the first open car up Broadway, followed by players and their wives in others. Crowds pressed against them, people threw the traditional ticker tape and torn newspapers from windows.

"A-gee, A-gee, A-gee," screamed a group of youngsters perched on a government building balcony and Tommie acknowledged the greeting with a wave and a smile.

"Hey Gil," yelled a fan to Hodges. "Have them put the roof down on your car. We don't want you to get hurt. We want you for next year."

"Gosh, there are more people here on one street corner than in my whole town. This is incredible." That's the way Jim McAndrew, the 25-year-old pitcher from Lost Nation, Iowa (pop, 537) described "the biggest day of my life."

Ed Kranepool, the only home-bred New Yorker, from the Bronx, said, "I've never seen such a large and enthusiastic crowd. But the fans deserve this day. They're the No. 1 fans in the No. 1 town in the world."

After the City Hall ceremony the motorcade took the astronauts' route up Park Avenue, then to Bryant Park, where more ceremonies were held by *Hello Dolly*'s Pearl Bailey. Later came the reception at Gracie Mansion by Mayor and Mrs. Lindsay.

The Mets became the most rhapsodized and sought-after collection of over-achievers in the country.

The city's campaigning Mayor John Lindsay, eager to identify himself with a winner, first proclaimed the following Monday New York Mets Day, then renamed Brooklyn's famed Bedford Avenue for Mets manager Gil Hodges.

The Mets' World Series shares amounted to approximately $15,000 apiece. Soon the extra loot, and opportunities to make same, began to pour in.

A large ad on the advertising pages of the papers appeared reading:

"Now available. Tom Seaver, America's top athlete and sports personality. Plus—Nancy Seaver, Tom's lovely wife, for those situations that call for young Mrs. America or husband and wife sales appeal."

Tom and Nancy Seaver appeared on the "Kraft Music Hall" TV special, where Tom fielded a pie with his face and sang "Nancy With the Laughing Face."

An official of Mattgo Enterprises, Inc., the personal management firm, estimated that the Seavers could make "about $250,000" during the off-season.

"By next spring there won't be one major variety or talk show that hasn't had an appearance by a Met," said agent Frank Scott, who represents most of the players. "The Mets will make more as a group than any team in history; they'll maybe divide $400,000."

Seven of them signed for a two-week stand at Caesar's Palace, one of the many plush Las Vegas night spots, at $5,000 per week. Reviewed *Variety*, the theatrical trade weekly:

"Song, dances, comedy and novelty are spotlighted in the new Caesar's Maximus offering—the songs and music are tossed by Jimmy Rodgers and Terry Rinaldi, the comedy comes from Dick Van Dyke and Phil Foster and seven of the New York Mets (Tom Seaver, Tom Agee, Cleon Jones, Donn Clendenon, Art Shamsky, Jerry Koosman and Ed Kranepool) are there for the novelty.

"It was inevitable that some agent would sign some Mets to a vaude contract and offer the world champions to niteries and theatres.

"Several years ago Milton Berle brought six of the champion Brooklyn Dodgers—Maury Wills, Don Drysdale, Duke Snider, Sandy Koufax, Frank Howard, and Willie Davis—with him to the Desert Inn and the carefully rehearsed act turned out to be a pleasant surprise.

"Unfortunately the seven Mets don't have an act. Tux-clad, with numbers in white on their backs, the players seem ill at ease while singing 'Impossible Dream' (eyeing idiot cards) and their jokes are spoiled by confusion with punchlines. Only Phil Foster, the old pro, who guides them around the stage, gets yocks with every line.

"However baseball fans will appreciate the color film clip of the 'Ex-Mets,' showing some funny ineptness with dropped balls, players crashing together and beaned batters, then the 'now' hero Mets and highlighting the Series at Shea Stadium.

"To bookers considering the act—insist that the boys bring along the movies." Anyway, the Mets were the only act in Las Vegas to bring down the house without taking their clothes off.

Meanwhile Ron Swoboda was off for a tour of Viet Nam with a USO troupe. Ron Taylor, Tug McGraw and others were to follow later.

Maybe Casey Stengel, the celebrated Last Word, put it best when, at the victory wingding in the Diamond Club after that final game, he said:

"This is a team which has come along slowly fast. . . . Gimme another pineapple juice and vodka."

APPENDIX:

THE DAY THEY INVENTED THE METS

The Mets were spawned in the summer of 1959 by the Continental League, a proposed third major league originated by William A. Shea, a New York attorney who had been appointed by New York's Mayor Robert F. Wagner to explore possibilities of bringing another major league baseball club to the country's largest city.

The Continental, which was to have included Toronto, Buffalo, Houston, Denver, Atlanta, Dallas–Fort Worth, Minneapolis–St. Paul and New York, never got off the ground but it remained in the running for a little over a year.

Shea and Branch Rickey, the inspirational 81-year-old president of the league, in their efforts to get the Continental going, stormed Congress seeking anti-trust legislation. The Senators turned it down, but the move scared the operators of American and National League franchises, and in August, 1960, they decided to expand to 10 clubs apiece. The American beat the National to it by a year, the latter voting to add New York and Houston, though not until the start of the 1962 season.

Mrs. Charles Shipman Payson (the former Joan Whitney and sister of John Hay Whitney) was the principal backer of the Continental's no-name New York club. Others were Dwight Davis, Jr., G. Herbert Walker, Jr., William Simpson and M. Donald Grant, the latter known as Mrs. Payson's "minister of finance."

When the Continental disbanded and the New York entry was accepted, along with Houston, by the National League, it was supposed that Rickey would head the New York group. He decided against moving to New York, however, and the only baseball man left in sight was Charles Hurth, former president of the Southern League, who had been made the New York general manager on Rickey's recommendation.

Grant, a senior partner in the leading Wall Street house of Fahnestock & Co., had bought one share of stock in the New York Giants for Mrs. Payson some 20 years before. Later she increased it to ten per cent. Grant, who represented her baseball interests then as now, was the only member of the board of directors to vote against the Giants' move to San Francisco. He had, in fact, sought to purchase the club from Horace Stoneham on behalf of Mrs. Payson to keep it in New York.

Now he needed a top-drawer baseball man to head the organization and immediately thought of George Weiss, the quiet, soft-spoken Connecticut Yankee who had long established himself as one of the game's shrewdest operators. Weiss had been retired by the Yankees a few days after Stengel and had nothing to do but roam around his Greenwich home all day—prompting his wife Hazel to complain: "When I married George it was for better or worse . . . but not for lunch. He just has to get a job. In baseball, or not, but a job."

After a number of meetings with Grant and one in Florida with Mrs. Payson, he agreed to take over as president of the club. It was starting from scratch. He had no proven players, no ball park, no organization and no manager.

Weiss's first official act was to sign Johnny Murphy, the one time Yankee relief pitcher and former head of the Boston Red Sox farm system, to scout New England territory. Later Murphy was named administrative assistant.

Hurth, the Rickey man, was permitted to resign. Grant became chairman of the board. Held over from the Continental setup were Wid Mathews, who had been scouting in the West and whom Weiss made his Western administrative assistant; Matt Burns, a former Brooklyn Dodger front-office man; Margaret Regetz, a former Yankee secretary who now became Weiss's; and Lou Niss, a public relations man who was made road secretary.

Tom Meany, a former sportswriter and author who had also worked for Weiss on the Yankees, was named public relations director. Jim Thomson, who had been superintendent of Yankee Stadium under him, was put in charge of the Polo Grounds, which was leased from the city until the new stadium being built in Flushing Meadows was ready. Bill "The Judge" Gibson, who had worked at Ebbets Field for years, was made ticket manager.

Put in command of the press lounge was Bill Boylan, who after pitching for York and other clubs in the old New York–Pennsylvania League for years, had become a Brooklyn milk man. After he finished his morning route Bill used to park the truck outside Ebbets Field, go into the Brooklyn clubhouse, put on a uniform and pitch batting practice for Babe Herman, Chick Fewster and other Dodger greats of the day.

On an early October morning Casey Stengel was in the vault of the Valley National Bank in Glendale California counting his money when the phone rang. It was Weiss asking him to manage the club. Later Casey was heard to say why he finally agreed: "Weiss kept calling me up on the phone so often, interruptin' my bankin', then he put Mrs. Payson on the phone an' I decided when a nice person like her wanted me an' was willin' to put all that money behind the club I couldn't say no."

Stengel flew to New York for signing ceremonies, then returned to California where he began talking up his new club—frequently referring to them as the "Knickerbockers" instead of calling them the Mets. Soon he was back in New York again, riding a special Mets float in Macy's Thanksgiving Day parade.

Next came the job of stocking the Mets and the Houston club with players from the other National League clubs by a form of draft. The plan called for each of the other clubs to designate 15 players. The new clubs were to take two players at $75,000 apiece from each of the eight clubs; then, if they chose, another player at $50,000 from each club and finally no more than four designated as premium players at $125,000 per man.

Weiss had already moved to build a sound coaching and scouting staff. Rogers Hornsby, who was to become the Mets' special batting instructor, had been watching all major league games in Chicago and filed reports on more than 400 players, some of whom might be put on the National League draft list.

Cookie Lavagetto, who had been fired as Minnesota manager the previous season, was hired to observe National League games in San Francisco. When Solly Hemus was dismissed as manager of the St. Louis Cardinals he was asked to scout the games in Los Angeles. Murphy, meanwhile, was scouting the men National League clubs had sent down for experience in the top minors. Then they all met with Weiss and went over the combined list of potential draftees.

They picked Gil Hodges, the first baseman from the Dodgers; Elio Chacon, an infielder from the Reds; Hobie

Landrith, a catcher from the Giants; Don Zimmer, a third
baseman from the Cubs; Felix Mantilla, an infielder from
the Braves; Joe Christopher, an outfielder from the Pirates; Lee Walls, an outfielder–first baseman from the
Phils; Gus Bell, an outfielder from the Reds; Ed Bouchee,
a first baseman from the Phillies; and pitchers Jay
Hook of the Reds, Roger Craig of the Dodgers, Ray
Daviault of the Giants and Al Jackson, Bob Miller and
Craig Anderson of the Cardinals. All this at a cost of
$1,800,000.

Then they filled the roster by sending Walls and
$125,000 to the Dodgers for Infielder Charley Neal; buy-
ing Frank Thomas, an outfielder, from the Braves; Richie
Ashburn, another outfielder, from the Cubs; and buying
provisionally, Clem Labine, Johnny Antonelli and Bill
Loes. The last two decided to quit baseball before the
following season opened. They also added outfielders
Bobby Gene Smith, Jim Hickman and John DeMerit, plus
catchers Joe Ginsberg and Clarence (Choo Choo) Coleman.

Unlike the Houston club, which drafted young, virtual
unknowns, the Mets went after older, more experienced
players like Hodges, Thomas, Bell, Neal and Bouchee who
might be useful hitters in the Polo Grounds. They were
also name players who figured to help attract old National
League fans to the park.

To Branch Rickey it seemed that Mrs. Payson had been
gyped, that she had been allowed to have only the poorest
material by the eight other owners and was really paying
$8 million for what amounted to an initiation fee. He said
the Mets had gathered together players who had passed
their prime and were "about to go down the other side of
the hill."

"It's clear we can't just stand still and wait for our
young players to develop," said Weiss at the time. "For

perhaps the first three years we may have to play with what you might call 'one-year men,' players only good enough for that length of time. By the end of that time we hope we'll be getting good results from our scouts and farm system."

In the beginning the Mets had only 15 untried youngsters, holdovers from the Continental League. Before the first spring they increased this number to 98—mostly free-agents, semi-pros and kids fresh from high school or college ball. Most were assigned to the four minor league clubs with which the Mets formed working agreements: Syracuse in the International League; Santa Barbara in Class C; Auburn, N.Y. and Quincy, Ill., in Class D. Before that first spring too, Lavagetto, Hemus, Red Kress, a former New York Giant coach, and Charley (Red) Ruffing, a former Yankee pitcher, had been named Stengel's coaches. Gus Mauch, who had served as the Yankees' trainer under Casey, was hired to soothe, rub and repair the Mets.

They also had a sizeable scouting system going for them with 36 scouts operating under Bill Bergesch, then the head of their new farm system.

Weiss negotiated what the trade called a terrific financial deal in selling the radio-TV rights to a beer company, Liebman Brothers, and a cigarette company Brown & Williamson, permitting them to televise a minimum of 126 games each year for five years. The contract signed with Liebman came to more than $6,000,000, the largest radio-TV deal ever made by a baseball club.

Also initiated were pre-game and post-game television shows produced by Joe Gallagher.

The Mets took early aim at the Long Island communities in their search for customers, believing that the Yankees had not exploited the territory for all it was worth after the Giants and Dodgers left town. Many of the old Ebbetts Field faithful had moved there and would be within easy reach of the new Mets stadium in Flushing Meadows.

Jim Murray, who had pitched for the Dodgers briefly, and Betty King, who had been in the Yankee organization, were assigned to develop interest in the Mets in the Long Island communities, organizing group expeditions to games by women's organizations and other clubs.

The Mets are probably the only ball club that ever sold tickets before it had any players.

In November of 1961 when the Mets were still more or less in the blue-print stage, they had a little office in the basement of the Martinique Hotel with Bill Gibson in charge. A sign over the door read:

"Mets' Ticket Office."

Bill said that every once in a while people would show up and ask for a couple of good seats for La Boheme or some other opera, and he'd have to direct them seven blocks north on Broadway. "I did my level best for the Metropolitan Opera Company," say Gibson. "I hope they had a reciprocal arrangement for me."

In October of 1961 the Polo Grounds looked like a Texas oil field. The city had eight drilling machines there taking borings for the imminent erection of a housing project planned for the site. Weiss met several times with New York City Housing Authority officials, who had already begun condemnation proceedings of the land around the old park. It was agreed to rent the place to the Mets while they waited for the new municipal stadium in Flushing Meadows to be completed.

The Mets also had to negotiate with the San Francisco Giants, who still owned the tower lights, seats and turnstiles, and were responsible for dismantling them. The club spent more than $300,000 fixing up the place, erecting a new scoreboard and resodding the field.

When the National League had held its expansion draft in October, 1961, the Mets owned nothing but 10 used baseballs, the donation of Johnny Murphy, left over from the tryouts that had been conducted for youngsters by the club in its Continental League days. Now they had an organization, a manager, players and a ball park. They were in business.

If you enjoyed this book, you will want to read these other absorbing TEMPO BOOKS

WILLIE MAYS, by Arnold Hano. Down in the 5337 75¢
dugout, out on the field . . . the closest look
yet at this American sports hero.

YAZ, by Carl Yastrzemski and Al Hirshberg. Yaz 5330 75¢
is a home-run hitting, hard-playing champion,
with the magnetism distinctive to all of baseball's greats. An exciting saga of a man who
may well become a legend.

BURIED TREASURE IN THE U. S. And Where to Find 5303 75¢
It, by Thomas Penfield. Exciting true tales of
pirates, prospectors and fabulous fortunes—
plus a list of 807 lost treasures.

ROD SERLING'S THE TWILIGHT ZONE. Weird tales 4789 60¢
of bizarre events too strange to be believed,
yet too grippingly real to be doubted.

ROD SERLING'S TWILIGHT ZONE REVISITED. A 4871 60¢
new collecting of startling explorations into
the realm of the supernatural.

BEETLE BAILEY, by Mort Walker. A zany col- 4884 75¢
lection from America's No. 1 comic strip,
starring Beetle Bailey and the funniest cast of
characters that ever turned an army camp
upside down.

FALL OUT LAUGHING, BEETLE BAILEY, by Mort 5305 75¢
Walker. More madcap misadventures starring Beetle Bailey and his fun-seeking friends
and foes.

THE PUSHCART WAR, by Jean Merrill. The his- 4804 60¢
torical (hysterical) story of New York's Pushcart War of 1976 . . . including the Daffodil
Massacre and the Pea Shooter Campaign.

SINBAD AND ME, by Kin Platt. A really smart 4861 50¢
English bulldog helps his master unravel mys-
teries in this hilarious puzzler.

TEST OF VALOR: A Story of the Ancient Olympic 4754 50¢
Games, by James Wesley Ingles. A magnificent young athlete pits himself against the
brutish Ajax in a vivid, suspenseful story.

GUIDE TO WHERE IT'S AT, by Bobbie Ashley. 4899 $1
Addresses of all your favorite people, like Bob
Dylan, Joan Baez, the Doors, Dustin Hoffman;
information on travel and study abroad; job
information; plus your own personal address
section.

FINE ART OF SPYING, edited by Walter B. Gib- 4849 50¢
son. A collection of nine true and truly unbelievable tales of espionage—some told by
the operatives themselves.

THE POISONED IVY, by William Surface. A 5000 95¢
shocking explosive report about students and
drugs in America's outstanding universities.

EASTERN RELIGIONS IN THE ELECTRIC AGE, by 4896 95¢
John H. Garabedian and Orde Coombs. The
controversial book about the moral revolt in
America—why millions of young people are
seeking new answers in the ideas and religions
of the East.

ATTACK FROM ATLANTIS, by Lester Del Rey. A 5306 75¢
startling science fiction adventure as timely as
today's headlines. An American atom sub van-
ishes and plunges the world into a new Cold
War crisis.

ROOSEVELT GRADY, by Louisa R. Shotwell. 4767 60¢
Roosevelt dreamed of living in one place where
he would not be an outsider, but for a migrant
worker's family, this wasn't easy.

THE STORY CATCHER, by Mari Sandoz. The 4790 50¢
moving story of how an Indian boy proved
himself a man in the eyes of his people.

HIGH ROAD HOME, by William Corbin. Evad- 4729 50¢
ing pursuers, living by his wits, Nico set forth
across the vast American continent in search
of his father.

NIGHT BEAT, by William Camp. As realistic as 5332 75¢
a documentary movie, NIGHT BEAT tells
what 3 policemen experience as they rush to
the scenes of action—action ranging from
the tension of a race riot to the poignance
of a lost child.

ANDY BUCKRAM'S TIN MEN, by Carol R. Brink. 4851 50¢
Andy builds four robots—then finds himself
marooned with them on a deserted island!

THE GNOMOBILE, by Upton Sinclair. The merry, 4812 50¢
madcap adventures of Elizabeth and Rodney
and two delightful gnomes in search of a home.

FRIDAY'S TUNNEL, by John Verney. The zany Cal- 4870 60¢
lendar family—an offbeat crew of eight—gets
caught up in an international crisis of intrigue
and espionage.

FEBRUARY'S ROAD, by John Verney. Another 5311 60¢
sparkling adventure—loaded with mirth and
mystery—starring the amazing Callendar family.

THREE MEN ON THIRD, by Gene Olson. When a 4826 50¢
wacky team has a coach who doesn't know a
home run from a hypotenuse, the ball game is
strictly for laughs.

and these HENRY REED books
by Keith Robertson

HENRY REED, INC. This serious journal of 4856 60¢
Henry's wildly funny business enterprises
makes a hilarious book.

HENRY REED'S JOURNEY. Henry's search for fire- 4857 60¢
works takes him and Midge on the funniest
coast-to-coast tour ever.

HENRY REED'S BABY-SITTING SERVICE. Henry 4858 60¢
could handle the babies, but a peacock really
makes the feathers fly!

If your dealer does not have the books you want, **ORDER**
from **TEMPO BOOKS,** 51 Madison Avenue, New York, N.Y.
10010 enclosing check or money order—no currency or
C.O.D.'s please. Please include 10¢ per book for postage and
handling. A complete list of titles is available free upon request.